Ski Patroller

Ski Patroller

Can You Make the Grade?
Would You Like the Work?

Michael Commins

Foreword by Jim Chase

STACKPOLE BOOKS

Published by
STACKPOLE BOOKS
Cameron and Kelker Streets
P.O. Box 1831
Harrisburg, PA 17105

Printed in the United States of America

10 9 8 7 6 5 4 3 2 1

First Edition

All photographs by the author unless otherwise noted

Illustrations by Richard "Gizmo" Getzlaff

Cover photo by Wade H. McKoy

Cover design by Tracy Patterson

Interior design by Marcia Lee Dobbs

Library of Congress Cataloging-in-Publication Data

Commins, Michael.
   Ski patroller : can you make the grade? Would you like the
work? / Michael Commins. – 1st ed.
     p.   cm.
   Includes bibliographical references.
   ISBN 0-8117-2363-1
   1. Skis and skiing – Vocational guidance. I. Title.
GV854.C5918   1990
796.93'023 – dc20
                                   89-48257
                                      CIP

This book is dedicated to
Bill, Caroline,
and most of all,
to Karen

Contents

Foreword

Everybody knows that ski patrollers get to ski for free. Of course, deep inside we all know that there's a lot more to it, but that seems to be the one thing that all skiers remember first: Ski patrollers ski all over the mountain, all day, for free. What gets lost somewhere is what these people are actually doing. We forget, for example, what skiing was like before there was ski patrol; we conveniently banish all thoughts of the daredevil, death-defying image that skiing used to have back in the days when you took your life and your limbs into your hands every time you pushed off down the slopes. But think about it for a moment: People used to die doing this. They used to suffer terrible disabilities simply because they fell and hurt themselves with their old bindings and low boots, and there was nobody to help them – at least nobody who knew what they were doing.

True, skiing will always be a risk sport to some degree. What can you expect when you strap slippery skids with metal edges onto your feet, climb a steep hillside, stand on frozen water, and let gravity take its course? However, it is far, far safer these days than in the benighted '30s. Deaths are infrequent now (even though there are literally millions more skiers than there were fifty years ago), and they are invariably caused by some fool disobeying a ski patroller by skiing too fast or stepping out of bounds. And best of all, injured skiers recover far faster and more completely simply because their rescuers get there quickly and are skilled enough not to make a bad situation any worse.

But the main thing that skiers don't usually realize about their friends with the fanny packs around their waists and the crosses on the middle of their backs is the simple, fundamental truth of a ski patroller's life: These folks work like hell. They start early, they work late, and they rarely slow down in between. Those patrollers skiing down the slope aren't out on a lark. They're in transit between one job and another, whether it be tobogganing an injured skier to the bottom, marking a hazard, closing an avalanche chute (or bombing it with hand-delivered explosives), or performing that old patrol favorite: chewing out some young yahoo for endangering society, and receiving copious lip in return. Later on they'll miss their dinners searching around the bushes in the dark for a lost skier.

The skills of the ski patrol are impressive, as are the day-to-day tasks they perform unnoticed. Even more impressive though, are the spirit and commitment with which these are done. If you think you might like to join a ski patrol (as a volunteer or as a professional) or if you'd just like to know a little more about it, the seemingly endless particulars of a ski patroller's life make exciting, fascinating, and, in a funny way, inspiring reading. Perhaps knowing the patrollers' story will make you feel just a bit more a part of this exciting sport, which enriches our lives so much; perhaps you'll simply gain a better appreciation of the contribution that the ski patrol makes to that sport. But never again will you see a couple of ski patrollers slide by and think, "Aw, they're just skiing for free."

Jim Chase
Managing Editor, *Skiing* magazine

Acknowledgments

Many thanks to all the patrollers, lift operators, and staff at Grand Targhee Resort and elsewhere who helped me get the photographs for this book. Thanks also to Alicia Leppert and Judy Bunce at National Ski Patrol headquarters, and to Jon Stuart and Mary Downey at Mountain Camera Supply in Jackson, Wyoming.

Thanks most of all to Karen Commins for her encouragement, criticism, support, and proofreading.

An Important Note to Readers

The purpose of this book is to inform and entertain. Since many of the patrolling techniques that it describes involve risks, you should not attempt them without proper instruction and supervision. Those techniques include but are not limited to: handling a toboggan, evacuating a ski lift (including self-evacuation), searching for lost skiers, and reducing the hazards of an avalanche. The book may serve as a training guide for new patrollers, but it cannot replace thorough instruction by qualified patroller-trainers.

There are over six hundred ski areas in the United States, and, of course, not all ski patrols do everything the same way. This book describes, however, the basic techniques that a beginning patroller will learn at almost any ski area. Advanced techniques are beyond the scope of this book.

1

A Day's Work
at a Small Ski Resort

You've seen ski patrollers at work – they're the ones on the slopes wearing jackets with white or yellow crosses. You know their job is to rescue injured skiers and you see them ski a lot. If you think that's all they do, this book will give you a better picture of what a ski patroller's job entails. The work ranges from boring to exciting and often switches unexpectedly from one to the other. Part of every day, a ski patroller sits in some shack, wearing ski boots and waiting for telephone calls. It can be very dull. But when the phone rings and a voice on the other end says, "We've got someone hurt down here and we need a patroller quick," a patroller's adrenaline starts to flow. He rushes out the door, grabs a toboggan, and heads for the accident scene.

Volunteer and professional ski patrollers have two things in common: a love of skiing and a desire to help others. For the person who loves skiing, no other job, in my opinion, offers more opportunity to enjoy the sport. Most patrollers start because of their desire to ski but stay on for the satisfaction of helping injured skiers. Few jobs can match the satisfaction patrolling offers – the satisfaction of knowing that someone you rescued is well and is skiing again.

Volunteer ski patrollers come from as wide a range of backgrounds as do skiers. Doctors, lawyers, engineers, business people, and individuals from just about every other occupation imaginable can be found patrolling ski slopes.

Professional patrollers tend to be independent types who aren't out to get rich – they enjoy the seasonal nature of the job. One Copper Mountain, Colorado, patroller ships out as a crew member on ocean racing yachts when ski season ends. Dozens spend their summers as river rafting or fishing guides, while hundreds of pro patrollers catch up financially through summer construction work.

National Ski Patrol volunteers dedicate their winter weekends to helping the skiing public at no charge, while professional patrollers often work for little more than minimum wage. They get free skiing for themselves and their families, along with some discounts in the ski shop or cafeteria. But the long hours and hard work soon prove that old saying, "There's no such thing as a free lunch."

To illustrate what your day might be like as a ski patroller, let's imagine you are a patroller at a small ski area, and we'll follow you through a day on the job.

————————◆————————

Your alarm rings at 5:00 a.m., and you struggle out of bed. It's been snowing and blowing all night. Today's your day to get to the ski area early and check the weather conditions. Last night when you went to bed, there were a couple of inches of new snow on the hood of your car; now you can barely see the car. It will be a great day for skiing but you wonder how you'll get your car out of the driveway.

Usually the drive to work takes half an hour, but today you'll need at least an hour to shovel out and drive through the thick snow. It's a good thing the snowplows are out. They're concentrating on the streets in town, though, and the closer you get to the ski area, the deeper the snow on the road gets. By the time you reach the parking lot, your car barely pushes ahead even though the snow is light and dry.

You trudge through the parking lot to the ski patrol locker room where you check the wind chart on the recording anemometer. Two jagged red lines on a moving chart show you the wind speed and direction for the night – it averaged about twenty miles an hour out of the southwest, with gusts to thirty miles an hour.

Next, you warm up a snowmobile and drive to the weather station to check the snow depth and water content. Eighteen inches of new snow have fallen overnight with one and a half inches of water content. Dumping the snow off the "twenty-four-hour stake," you check the total snow depth and the maximum and minimum temperatures. You'll write down all the weather figures when you get back to the ski patrol locker room.

A telephone conversation with the ski patrol director confirms what the director and the rest of the patrol discussed at the end of the day yesterday: you'll be performing avalanche hazard reduction using explosive charges.

It's your responsibility to telephone the rest of the patrollers scheduled for the day and tell them the plan. Most are already awake, but one is still asleep when you call. You can't resist giving him a bad time.

"Hey, wake up," you say. "We've got work to do."

"Yeah, okay. Give me a minute," says the sleepy voice.

"Hey, I've been up for an hour. Get out of that bed!"

After a long yawn, he mutters, "Yeah, okay, see you in a while."

After phoning all the patrollers, you grab a two-way radio and the keys to the explosives storage, then go back outside to the snowmobile. Snowflakes spit out of the darkness into the headlight beam as you steer the snowmobile toward the explosives shack. The wind is still blowing hard – it's whistling through the big fir trees as you unlock the steel door of the explosives shack. It's 6:30 a.m. You sign for a box of two-pound cast primers on the records sheet, and with the explosives strapped to the snowmobile, you head back to the locker room with enough explosives to make a ten-foot-wide crater in the ground.

Back inside the locker room, you begin preparing the fuses and the blasting caps. You start by cutting lengths of orange "safety fuse" according to a mark on the bench. As you begin to crimp the blasting caps onto the fuse ends, the ski patrol director arrives. He goes directly to the wind recorder and looks at the record of last night's wind.

"Looks like a good one this morning," the director says as he rolls the wind chart back onto its spring-loaded roller.

"Yeah. I can't wait to make some turns in that stuff."

"Should be some good skiing if the wind doesn't get it," he says, "but we might have some slab action up high."

He glances at the wind recorder. "Days like this make me glad this mountain isn't steep all over. A few steep spots are enough."

The prospect of eighteen inches of wind-driven snow on the mountain's steep spots propels the two of you to finish the explosives preparation. There's a real possibility that you'll start some avalanches today. You crimp caps onto all the fuses, then insert a cap and fuse into the hole in each two-pound primer. By the time the rest of the ski patrol begins arriving, the "bombs" are in rucksacks and ready to go.

The arrival of more patrollers in the small locker room increases the noise level, and the excitement builds. As everyone changes into ski clothes and ski boots, there are four or five separate conversations going on at once.

Soon all the patrollers are ready, and before going out the door, several patrollers recite a short litany: "Skis boots poles, hats goggles gloves radio, Pieps shovel pack." In the rush to get ready, it's easy to forget some vital piece of equipment.

When you get to the loading ramp, the lift operators are furiously shoveling snow. They stop long enough to greet the advancing patrollers and begin chuckling when they spot the patrol director. When you see what they're laughing at, you laugh too and then quickly pretend to concentrate on putting on your skis.

"What's so funny?" the patrol director asks of no one in particular.

A lift operator points at the patrol director's head.

"Your goggles are on upside down."

"What's the matter, Mike?" yells another lift operator. "Have too much fun last night?"

Soon everyone is laughing as the patrol director takes his goggles off and puts them back on right side up.

"Just checking to see if anyone would notice," he says as he gets on the lift.

As you ride up the lift, you talk with your partner about the possible conditions on your avalanche control route. "Maybe the skiing to the route won't be so great today."

"Yeah. It's hard to tell from here, though – could be good in the trees where the wind didn't get to it." Daylight is coming on slowly and the snowflakes seem to have thinned out, but you can see that thick clouds blanket the top half of the mountain and the wind continues blowing.

About halfway up the lift, you ascend into the fog and wind. The snow has turned to graupel – little pellets of snow that sting when they hit your face – and the fog reduces the visibility to about fifty feet. The patrol gathers at the top of the lift, and a few patrollers take their personal rucksacks into the ski patrol summit shack. The avalanche hazard reduction teams pair up, and you and your partner head out to "The Chutes," your avalanche route.

Each of you carries twenty pounds of explosives in rucksacks, and as you start toward your route, the wind drives the graupel into your face. Head down, you follow your partner's tracks. After traversing into the wind for half a mile, you are above The Chutes. You attempt a few turns in the deep snow. The poor visibility, the heavy pack on your back, and the wind-packed snow all conspire to ruin any skiing style you may have had. You make about ten turns, barely avoiding a fall, before it's time to stop and traverse through The Chutes.

"Good skiing, eh?" your partner says as he takes two bombs out of your pack.

"I've had better," you answer. "I just about crashed up there."

He hands one of the bombs to you. "I kind of liked it. It's cream cheese snow."

"I'll get the hang of it, I guess. I plan to ski a lot today."

Your partner chuckles. "You'll be too tired for much skiing if we have to help cut cornice this morning," he says.

"Naw, I'm never too tired to ski powder," you say, shaking your head.

A ski patroller uses an underhand toss to place a "two-pounder" (*upper left center*) in an avalanche starting zone. The string keeps the bomb from rolling down a hard snow surface.

SKI PATROLLER

"Yeah. Well, we better get started." Your partner nods in the direction of a chute. "Throw yours right below us, and I'll put mine just over there below those trees."

You each get fuse lighters out of your pockets and slip them onto the ends of the fuses. Your partner counts to three. On three, you both give the igniters a sharp pull, push them down on the fuses quickly, and give the bombs underhand tosses downhill. You look at your watch, noting the position of the second hand. Then you both traverse quickly toward a group of trees in the direction of your next chute. In the relative safety of the trees, you wait until your watch says there are thirty seconds left before the bombs explode. Then you both put your hands over your ears.

The last thirty seconds always take forever, you think to yourself, but finally you see one gray and white plume of snow, then another, come up the hill a split second before the noise of the blast reaches you. Then you both traverse to a spot that lets you see if any avalanches resulted. You get there in time to see moving snow piling up about ten feet deep and fifty feet wide at the bottom of the two chutes.

"They won't be skiing powder in those chutes today," says your partner.

"Nope. Too bad, too. I might have been the first one back over here if it hadn't slid."

You continue with the rest of your route, and a few small avalanches result from the bombing. You finish quickly and return to the bottom of the lift just behind the other teams.

"Back to the top," the patrol director announces, "for cornice cutting."

The operators start the lift again, and the patrol boards. It is 8:45. The lifts open to the public at 9:30, giving the patrol forty-five minutes to ride the lift and cut the cornice. After unloading at the summit, all the avalanche teams ski to the ridge where the cornice forms.

This morning the cornice is huge. It overhangs about five feet and rolls down the ridge in white waves. The idea is to ski along the cornice, just the right distance from the edge, so the buildup of new snow falls away without taking the patroller with it. At first everyone is eager to lead the group, because the first one to cut a spot usually gets the biggest chunks of snow to fall. But today the snow is so deep and soft that skis submarine into it without breaking the cornice easily. Each time your skis dive, you are forced to lift them out by leg power. Even moving five feet ahead is a struggle. Despite the wind and twenty-degree temperature, you are soon sweating.

Occasionally a good-sized chunk of cornice falls away and everyone cheers when it does. One patroller gets too close to the edge and falls over the side with a chunk of snow. He's unhurt, but he's stuck below the cornice and is forced to traverse below the edge behind the rest of the crew. This happens almost every cornice-cutting day, and usually someone tries to knock a small chunk of snow down on the fallen patroller. The snow is soft and the chunks break up as they hit him, so it's harmless fun.

By 9:30 you've finished the cornice and returned to the bottom of the lift. A few skiers wait for the lift to open, and one asks, "How's the skiing?"

You jokingly tell him, "It's lousy – don't bother going up." The skier laughs.

Two patrollers cutting cornice.

The patrol boards the lift for the third time, just ahead of the first skiers.

In the patrol shack at the summit, you get a quick cup of coffee and the day's work assignments. The shack hardly has room for the small table, a few chairs, and two padded benches. Posters, pinups, and assorted magazine photos adorn the walls. A coffeemaker sits on a small shelf in one corner; another corner holds a telephone, a two-way radio, and a bookshelf. Two chalk boards on one wall show the day's assignments. Checking your assignment, you see that your run for the day is the "Ridge," and at 1:30 you will sit in the shack for an hour for accident coverage and communications. It's 10:00.

When you finish your coffee, you go out, put on your skis, and ski down the "Ridge." You look for the powder along the edges of the groomed snow. You almost ski by the first "Slow" sign. It's half buried and lying down on the edge of the run. All the slow signs are moved off the groomed snow each night so that if one does blow over and becomes partly buried, the grooming equipment won't run over it. You dig the sign out and stand it up in the middle of the run where it belongs. Continuing down, you put out the other two signs. Then near the bottom you see a hole where a grooming machine was stuck. You'll have to return with some bamboo poles and mark the hole so unwary skiers won't crash into it.

Back at the lift, you board with a skier. "Any broken legs today?" he asks, recognizing your ski patrol garb.

"No, we really don't see many broken legs, mostly sprained knees."

"Oh," the skier says, putting his goggles on his forehead. "That's good, I guess."

"Sometimes it is, but a sprained knee that needs surgery can take longer to heal than a broken leg."

As you pass the midway point of the chairlift, you go into the clouds. The skier puts his goggles, which have fogged up while on his forehead, down on his face. He can't see.

"You know, goggles seem to fog up worse when up on your forehead. You might try keeping them on your face while you ride the lift," you suggest. "Here, wipe them with this."

The skier wipes his goggles with your no-fog cloth. As he adjusts the goggles on his face, a gust of wind hits.

"It's kind of wild today," you say almost apologetically. "There's some good skiing, though, once you get out of the wind."

"Where can I do that?"

"Anywhere below the midway unloading station is good today. From the top, I'd go into the bowl. It's protected from the wind there, and the trees help you find your way down."

As the unloading ramp comes into view, the skier says, "I guess I'll try the bowl. That last run was too much for me."

You watch him disappear into the fog. Then you grab four bamboo poles from in front of the ski patrol shack. Holding the eight-foot-long poles in one hand and your ski poles in the other, you manage to make a few turns on your way to the hole you need to mark. When you get there, you jab the poles into the snow in an "X" pattern above the hole, then ski to the bottom of the lift. It's 10:30 and you're getting hungry. One more run, you decide. Then it'll be time for lunch.

This time no one is in the lift line, and you board the lift alone. As you settle into the ride and start to think about where you'll ski, the radio in your coat announces an accident.

"Summit to all patrol," the voice says. "There's a reported accident at the top of Big Bowl. Can anyone respond?"

Having just boarded the lift, you can't get there in a reasonable amount of time, so you don't respond to the call. No one else responds either, and soon the voice says, "We will cover it from the summit. KRB 584 clear."

Now your thoughts run to the reported accident. You wonder just where it is and who will respond. If they need extra help, you think, you might get to the summit just as they call for help. You've forgotten all about skiing powder, and as you pass the midway unloading ramp, the radio pipes up again.

"Five-four to summit."

"Summit here. Go ahead."

"I need a toboggan here. I'm about a third of the way down Big Bowl on the south side."

"Ten-four, summit copies. The toboggan is on its way. KRB 584 clear."

Sounds like they've got it covered, you think to yourself. If enough of them were on top having coffee, you'll still be able to make a run before lunch. The radio is quiet for the rest of the lift ride. Unloading at the summit, you go to the door of the patrol shack. Not wanting to take your skis off, you knock on the door with your ski pole.

"Need any help?" you ask the patroller who opens the door.

"Nope. Got three guys here. Go ahead and ski if you want."

Great, you think to yourself. You wonder why three patrollers are sitting in the shack on such a good powder day. Then you realize they are the three oldest members of the patrol. Those guys don't get excited about skiing unless it's *really* good, and today's fog and wind are enough to keep away all but diehard skiers.

You traverse to The Chutes, your avalanche control route. You know a run there that hardly ever gets skied, and you've been there so many times that the fog doesn't slow you down at all. You stop for a moment and look around. There are a couple of skiers below you who have come down a different chute. The clouds are above you, and the visibility is fairly good. You adjust your goggles, get a good grip on your ski poles, and drop into the chute.

You gain speed quickly in the steep chute, but the deep snow helps you maintain control. With every turn the snow flies in your face and over your

Skiing is a primary reason many people get into patrolling. Here two patrollers enjoy a powder day at Grand Targhee.

shoulders. You keep turning until the chute flattens out, then stop and look back at your tracks. Not bad, you think, and you push off to ski nonstop the rest of the way to the bottom of the mountain. You find powder most of the way, although in some places it's got quite a few tracks in it. All around, you hear skiers whooping in excitement. You reach the bottom of the lift just as another patroller is ready to board, and you ride up the lift with her.

"Been skiing yet, Megan?"

"No, I had top time right after we got done with the cornice. Then I went on a wreck."

"Oh yeah. I was on the lift when that call went out. What'd you find?"

"Sprained knee." Megan frowns, feeling sorry for the injured skier. "Where have you been skiing?"

"I've only had one free run so far. Skied The Chutes."

"How is it?"

"Great. It's a little wind-packed near the top, but once you get below the fog, there's some good skiing out there."

"I guess I'll go try it. Are you going back out there?"

It's 11:30 and you've been hungry for an hour. It's hard to turn down an invitation to ski, though, so you decide to take one more run before lunch.

You get off the lift and lead Megan to one of the less-traveled chutes. Just as you hoped, there are no tracks in it. You let her go first; then you make "figure-eights" out of her tracks.

"Show-off," she laughs.

The two of you make a nonstop run to the bottom, then get on the lift again and begin to ride to the top. About a third of the way up, the lift stops unexpectedly. Sometimes a skier has trouble loading or unloading, and the lift operator stops the lift while he helps the skier. Five minutes later, though, the lift still hasn't restarted, and you begin to wonder what the problem is.

"I've never evacuated from this high up," you say to Megan as you look down at the snow-covered ground fifty feet below.

"Me either," she replies. "I wonder what the holdup is."

Most of the time you don't think about the hundred-foot length of rope, the carabiner, and the webbing sling you carry in your first aid fanny pack. Now you are reassured by the bulge it makes against the small of your back, and you wonder if you should radio the summit and ask if they know anything about the lift.

Although you practice rappelling out of the lift every year, you've never done it in the fog and wind, high above the ground. Practice sessions are always near the bottom of the lift, where the chair is only fifteen feet above the ground. If the lift breaks down, you evacuate yourself first, then help evacuate skiers using a T-shaped seat and a rope much heavier than the one you carry.

Suddenly the lift starts again and you relax. You ride to the top and go inside the shack for lunch. Megan goes off to ski one more run.

Four or five patrollers are in the shack eating and listening to a tape of a new band. You join them with your bag lunch. By the time you finish eating it's 1:00. You have barely enough time to ski one run and get back to the top before your 1:30 summit duty.

Hurrying out, you put your skis on and ski nonstop down the ridge, checking the slow signs as you go. When you get back to the summit shack, there is only one patroller left, and he's dressed to go outside.

"Ready to go skiing?" you say.

"Yeah. Where's it good?"

"The Chutes," you call as he heads out the door.

You look around the room for something to read. You see some skiing magazines, some other old magazines that you've thumbed through and read a dozen times, and some outdoor equipment catalogs. You settle on a skiing magazine and start to read about skiing in Europe. It seems vaguely familiar. You've probably read it before.

The clock inches slowly toward two o'clock. You're not allowed to fall asleep or take your ski boots off. On a clear day, you could look out the window and watch skiers go by, but today you see nothing but fog and swirling snowflakes. You take a copy of the *Avalanche Handbook* off the bookshelf and thumb through it. Although there is always something new to learn in the *Avalanche Handbook,* this afternoon you feel too tired to tackle anything technical, so you sit and stare at the fog outside the window.

The ringing phone jolts you out of a daydream. The voice on the other end says, "This is midway. You got somebody hurt just above here. A skier came in and told me."

"Did they tell you what the problem is?" you ask.

"Nope. Didn't say right where it was, either – just said it's above here," the lift operator says.

"Okay. We'll get somebody there right away."

You grab the microphone of the two-way radio and announce, "Summit to all patrol. We have a reported accident just above midway. Can anyone respond?"

Every patroller on the mountain carries a radio, and anyone who can reach the accident will say so; otherwise the radio will remain silent. After a few seconds, the radio crackles.

"This is five-six. I can cover it."

"Ten-four, summit copies. Call if you need assistance. KRB 584 clear."

As you wait for the radio call, you buckle your ski boots and get ready to go outside. If there is an injury, you will need to bring a toboggan from the summit. If a patroller were on the lift anywhere close to the summit, they would have checked in over the radio. Finally the radio crackles.

"Five-six to summit."

"Summit here. Go ahead," you reply.

"I need a vacuum splint and a toboggan. I'm just above midway in the powder, south of the ridge."

"Ten-four, summit copies. Summit to all patrol: summit is now unattended." This means that the first patroller to reach the summit must go into the shack and take over communications.

You grab the vacuum splint in its rucksack, rush out the door, and strap the rucksack to a toboggan. The vacuum splint is used most often on dislocated shoulders, and you wonder if that's the injury. A dislocated shoulder is extremely painful and can result in permanent damage.

You take a few skating steps, pulling the toboggan behind you. Then you pick up speed and begin to concentrate on the slope ahead. You've grown used to skiing with the toboggan since you first started patrolling, and you make long sweeping turns down the groomed run. The toboggan follows in your wake, and your main concerns are to avoid skiers who might get in your way, and to find the crossed skis that will mark the accident. A group of skiers watch you ski by, and you feel a sudden rush of pride in your job. You continue, intent on finding the accident.

When you see the crossed skis marking the accident, the injured skier is sitting up and the patroller there is helping support the skier's right arm. You bring the toboggan in below them, stop with the toboggan across the fall line, and take your skis off. Then you plant your skis in the snow through the toboggan's handles, to prevent it from sliding away. You quickly get the vacuum splint out of its rucksack.

Jeff, the first patroller on the scene, tells you, "This gentleman's name is Bob, and he's dislocated his shoulder. He's most comfortable in the position he's in now."

Immediately you and Jeff work to get the splint under Bob's arm without moving the arm any more than necessary. The vacuum splint is a coated nylon bag filled with foam balls and fitted with a tire valve. A separate hand-operated pump sucks the air out of the bag, and atmospheric pressure on the foam balls causes the bag to become rigid in almost any shape. Nylon hook-and-pile straps allow the splint to be strapped on an injured person in a variety of ways.

Bob shudders and takes a deep breath when you move his elbow slightly to get the splint in place – you've made a mistake and caused him some pain.

"Sorry, Bob," you say. "I've got to get this splint under your arm."

"That's okay," Bob says. "Just get me out of here."

"We're almost ready. Just as soon as we get the air sucked out of this splint, we'll get you in the toboggan and head down the hill."

As Jeff pumps the air out of the splint, you turn your attention to the toboggan. The fiberglass toboggan contains a full-length pad, two blankets, and various splinting materials, all protected by a canvas cover. You arrange the pad and blankets with the unused splinting materials underneath. By now Jeff has finished pumping the air out of the splint, and you are ready to move Bob into the toboggan. In order to avoid moving him any farther than necessary, you bring the toboggan uphill until it's alongside Bob. You again plant skis through the handles so the toboggan can't go anywhere. Then you and Jeff help Bob get into the toboggan.

Lying down with a dislocated shoulder is usually very painful, so Bob will sit in the toboggan with his feet braced against the front. Jeff will also ride in the toboggan, sitting behind Bob and forming a human backrest. After Bob's and Jeff's skis are loaded in the toboggan, you put your skis on while Jeff holds the toboggan. Then while you hold the toboggan by the handles, Jeff gets in behind Bob, and you're ready to start downhill.

You look downhill, hoping to see some groomed snow just below you. You don't see any, but you judge from your position that there should be a cat track not too far below. With the weight of two people pushing you downhill in the powder, all you can do is sidestep in front of the toboggan. The chain brake under the front of the toboggan helps, but at times it stops the toboggan completely. Then you have to lift up the handles and pull the toboggan downhill to get it moving again.

After a couple of hundred yards, you reach the cat track and face a new problem – the slope of the cat track isn't steep enough for the toboggan to slide on its own. You tie the chain brake up out of the way and pull the toboggan down the cat track. About halfway down, a patroller skis by and helps you by pulling on the toboggan's tail rope.

As you near the bottom of the hill, your hands get unbearably cold while your upper body sweats. Your wrists, lower arms, and thighs burn from exertion. Approaching the first aid room, you're encouraged by the sight of two patrollers waiting to help you carry Bob inside. After bringing the double-loaded toboggan down two-thirds of the mountain, you doubt if you can hold up one end of a stretcher by yourself.

With Bob inside the first aid room and propped up on a bed, you again check his pulse while Jeff fills out the accident report form. Another patroller brings in the snow-covered blankets and pack cover, replaces them with dry ones, and folds everything inside the cover. Then he takes the toboggan to the bottom of the lift so it can be returned to the summit. You discover that Bob drove to the ski area alone, so you arrange for an ambulance to take him to the local hospital. It's 2:45.

You and Jeff gather up your skis and walk to the lift. When you get to the bottom of the lift, you stop to chat with the lift operator.

"Are you two ready for a lost kid tonight?" he says.

"No, why?" you answer.

"A guy came through asking if we'd seen his kid. Hasn't seen him since two o'clock."

"Where's the guy now?" Jeff asks.

"Went back up to look for him. The kid's not a very good skier, and the dad thinks he'll be able to find him if the kid is on the slopes."

"I wonder if the guy looked around the lodge."

"I think he did," says the lift operator. "Came up here without his skis. Then went to put them on. He seems pretty upset."

"Did you get his name or anything?" you ask.

"Kid's name is Billy. He's wearing a blue coat, black pants, red hat. Didn't get the dad's name."

"Where were they skiing?" asks Jeff.

"Bunny Run," says the lift operator.

"Well, it's still early," you say. "The kid could be skiing or somewhere in the lodge. Let's hope he's not lost."

"That's for sure."

"Tell the father if he still hasn't found the kid by four o'clock to call us," Jeff advises.

You both put your skis on and get on the lift. As you ride toward the top, you think about your last lost-person search. Jeff took part in that search, too. A woman and her husband got lost just a few weeks ago. They went past the ski area boundary, then began to quarrel over which way they should go. They split up. The husband retraced their tracks, but the wife took off through the timber. She thought it was a faster way back to the ski area. The husband made it back to the lodge at 5:00, just before the patrol normally leaves to go home. That search was relatively easy because there was a track to follow, and everyone knew from the start that it was the right track. The husband, riding on the back of a snowmobile, guided searchers to the point where the two split up. Then the patrollers followed her tracks.

She had traversed uphill through some thick trees up the side of a steep canyon. The patrollers followed her tracks for almost an hour before deciding that she would probably stay in the canyon, continuing in the same direction. They then called for a team of searchers to drop into the canyon from the ski area boundary. That team might cross a fresher track or make voice contact.

She cut just above some cliffs and avalanche chutes, almost got back into the ski area, then skied downhill. When the search team found her, she was near the bottom of an avalanche chute above some low cliffs. She was just a few hundred feet above the canyon floor, where a snowmobile could have picked them up, but the search team didn't feel it was safe to try and lower her down. The group was forced to climb up the steep chute back to the ski area. They made it back about 9:00. The lost woman was grateful and exhausted; her husband was relieved but annoyed.

"If this kid is lost," says Jeff, "it's going to be harder than that last search with the woman and her husband. This time we'll have to find a track."

"In this weather, a track a couple of hours old could be filled in by now."

"I think I'll ski along the boundary around Bunny Run and look for tracks," Jeff says.

"Good idea." You approach the top of the lift and get ready to unload. "I want to check my signs. Skiers have been knocking them over about this time of day, and I'd love to catch somebody in the act."

Jeff scowls. "I hate it when they do that. They wait till the end of the day because they know all you can do is take their lift tickets. It's their last run anyway, so what do they care?"

"At least I can read them the riot act." You smile at the prospect.

The top of the mountain is still shrouded in clouds, but the snow has stopped. Reaching the summit shack, you go in to get your ski poles (you didn't need them when you skied down with the toboggan), and Jeff suggests you ski together part way down.

You enjoy a leisurely pace at the beginning, but when you get out of the clouds where the visibility is better, you ski a little faster. You are forced to stop, however, when your thighs start to burn. The exertion of pulling the double-loaded toboggan has left you tired. You are just above the point where you and Jeff would split up anyway, so he continues down toward Bunny Run.

Looking for powder snow, you ski toward a run in the trees, which turns out to be a good choice because few skiers have been there ahead of you, and the snow looks good. You pick up speed, drop into the run, and immediately take an eggbeater fall. Snow is down your coat collar, inside your goggles, and one ski is off. You quickly look around – luckily, no one saw you. You wipe the snow out of your goggles the best you can, then struggle uphill to look for your ski. After searching in the deep snow for several minutes, you find it.

You continue past your slow signs, pleased to find them in place, and ski to the bottom on the groomed run without any further problems. But when you get to the lift, the lift operators notice the snow clinging to your hat. They can't resist a chance to give patrollers a bad time, and the snow on your hat is a dead giveaway.

"Looks like you've been skiing a little close to the trees or something," the operator says with a grin.

"Right, John. At least that's what you can tell everybody," you reply.

When you reach the summit, you go inside the patrol shack to wait for "sweep."

All of the patrol is already in the shack. The talk is mostly about lost persons and the day's skiing. You ask about the lost kid.

"They found him," says one patroller.

"That's good. Where was he?"

"Out skiing. Turns out he was more adventurous than his dad thought he was. He went to the rope tow while dad was looking for him on the beginner chair lift."

"Great," you sigh, sinking into a chair. "I wasn't too excited about a night search tonight."

"Neither was I," chorus five voices.

Some of the others begin leafing through magazines or reading books, but a couple, like you, sit and doze. You're startled awake every couple of minutes by someone's laughter or loud comment. Finally it's time to start sweep. There's a rush to get on coats, hats, gloves, and goggles, and to grab rucksacks and water bottles.

Sweep is the last run of the day. After the lifts close, the patrol skis down and tries to make certain no one is left on the mountain. That can be difficult on foggy days, and you end up shouting into the fog and hoping you'll be able to hear if anyone shouts back. One or more patrollers, known as "Supersweep," stay at the summit in case a patroller finds an injured skier on sweep.

One by one patrollers go out the door and get into their skis. You head for The Ridge, stopping every few hundred feet to shout "sweep" into the fog. Each time, you listen for a moment, then continue. As you come to signs in the run, you put them off the groomed area so the grooming machines won't run over them. About halfway down you get below the fog. The clouds seem to be breaking up, although they often break up at five o'clock only to fill back in again by midnight.

Near the bottom, you have a "wave-off" – a spot where you meet a patroller from another sweep run. The other patroller hasn't made it yet so you stop and wait. Poking through the clouds, the sun lights up a section of mountain. It's the first time the sun has come out all day.

The other patroller comes along, and you both wave as he continues down the rest of his run. Then you start down the last part of yours. It's part of the beginner area, and you ski slowly, looking into the trees on both sides. The tree areas are laced with paths made by kids. They love to ski in groups, following each other through the trees, the more twisted the route the better. You don't see or hear anything there, and finally you arrive in front of the locker room. It's 5:00 as you take off your skis and carry them inside.

The locker room is almost as noisy as it was in the morning. Ski boots are dropped on the floor and ski pants hung up to dry. There is talk of stopping at the lodge for a cold drink. It sounds like a great idea – it's been a long day.

Sometimes the scenery alone makes patrolling worthwhile.

2

Ski Patrollers: History, Standards, and Gear

I n 1521, Swedish soldiers on skis used reindeer hides stretched between pairs of skis to transport their injured.* They were the first to use a concept that has evolved into the modern ski patrol's workhorse – the toboggan with long handles. Skiing in Sweden and Norway has long been a way of life, and Swedes and Norwegians can be credited with bringing skiing to the rest of Europe, North America, and Australia. The earliest known European skiing outside of Scandinavia took place in 1868, when Norwegians took skis to the Alps. Then in 1892, an Austrian named Mathias Zdarsky invented the snowplow technique.** It was the first skiing technique that beginners could easily learn, and Zdarsky's ski school helped propel skiing's popularity in Europe.

Around the same time, Norwegian immigrants brought their knowledge of skiing to North America. Miners in Colorado, Utah, and California were among the most avid skiers in those days, and jumping became a popular spectator sport in the Midwest around the turn of the century. In California's Sierra Nevada, miners invented the dual race format and speed skiing races popular today. The miners raced four abreast straight down the mountain on ten-foot-long, handmade skis, often reaching a speed of eighty miles per hour. We can only imagine the spectacular accidents they must have had. Those early skiers were hardy individualists who took skiing's hazards as part of life.

By the 1930s skiing's popularity was growing in both Europe and North America. Around 1935, informal ski patrols – formed by expert skiers to help increasing numbers of skiers – turned up in California's Sierra Nevada, in the Cascade Range of Oregon and Washington, and in Central Montana.

---

* Besser, Gretchen R., *The National Ski Patrol: Samaritans of the Snow* (Woodstock, Vt.: The Countryman Press, 1983), 16.

** Dudley, Charles, *60 Centuries of Skiing* (Brattleboro, Vt.: Stephen Daye Press, 1935), 38.

The mountains of the eastern United States also saw growing numbers of skiers each year. At Mt. Mansfield, Vermont, skiing pioneer Roland Palmedo organized one of the first ski patrols in the East during the winter of 1935-36. Palmedo modeled the Mt. Mansfield patrol after the Swiss Parsenndienst at Davos, but with one distinction. The Swiss ski patrol charged for its services – the Americans did not. This difference still exists. Professional patrollers in the United States are paid by the resorts out of lift ticket proceeds, and volunteer patrols rely on fund-raising efforts, donations, and membership fees. Anyone who skis in the United States or Canada can expect ski patrol services free of charge.

In January 1936 at Stowe, Vermont, skier and insurance salesman C. Minot "Minnie" Dole broke his ankle while skiing. His friends dragged him off the mountain on a piece of roofing tin they found. Later that same year Frank Edson, who helped rescue Dole, died of a punctured lung that resulted from a skiing

A patroller needs top skiing skills to take a toboggan anywhere skiers might be hurt.

accident. Dole and a few skiing friends began to think of a nationwide rescue organization that could help prevent ski accidents and train skiers in safety, first aid, and rescue techniques. The National Ski Patrol was officially founded in 1938, and by 1941 it had grown to 180 ski patrols with 4,000 members.

Today there are almost 600 ski areas across the United States, and over 150 in Canada. Estimates place the number of skiers in the United States between 6.7 million and 18 million. At 25,000 members the National Ski Patrol now ranks as the world's largest winter rescue organization. It provides training, testing, and educational programs for virtually every volunteer ski patrol and for many professional ski patrols in the United States. Ninety percent of National Ski Patrol's members are volunteers, but the recently formed Professional Division attracts increasing numbers of professional patrollers to membership in the National Ski Patrol.

If you're a skier with a full-time career who likes to help others, volunteering on a ski patrol might be for you. Perhaps you can only afford a few weekends of skiing per season and prefer to do it with your kids. On the other hand, maybe you have more time to ski and would enjoy helping other skiers through patrol work.

Most small and medium-sized ski areas in the United States depend on the services of volunteer ski patrollers. Most large resorts use professional patrols, although a few have patrols made up of both professionals and volunteers. For example, Winter Park, Colorado, in 1987 boasted twelve double chairlifts, three triple chairs, and three quad chairlifts. On weekends and holidays in 1987 the Winter Park Ski Patrol typically consisted of thirty-two professionals, twenty-five volunteers, and ten "Junior Patrollers." The Junior Patroller program encourages younger skiers (the minimum age for adult patrollers is eighteen) to learn first aid and other ski patrol skills, assist adult patrollers, and carry the message of safe skiing to their peers.

Standards Required of Patrollers

As a prospective volunteer patroller, you will first be required to pass a ski test at the area where you would like to patrol. The tests are often held during the spring so training of qualified candidates can start the following fall. Ski patrolling demands top skiing skills, although you don't need the same type of mastery as a ski instructor. A pretty skiing style is not necessary for skiing down icy slopes with an armload of bamboo, answering accident calls in bad weather, or taking part in the early morning avalanche control. As a patroller, you will be expected to ski in all kinds of weather and snow conditions. The standards used for ski tests vary according to each ski area's terrain and conditions. Generally, if you are a strong parallel skier familiar with the area where you would like to patrol, you have a good chance of passing that patrol's ski test.

A few basic skiing skills that many advanced skiers pay little attention to should also be on your list of strong points: the snowplow, the hockey stop, and sideslipping.

Snowplow. Patrollers use the snowplow extensively for guiding loaded toboggans on moderate slopes. You should be able to hold a snowplow position for long distances on a moderate slope, staying in the fall line and stopping or turning at will. Practice until you can snowplow on a groomed run for three hundred yards without stopping.

Hockey Stop. The hockey stop demonstrates that you ski in control and can stop quickly to avoid another skier, provide aid at an accident, or stop with an empty toboggan. You should be able to turn into the hill, set your edges quickly, and come to a stop on any slope at any speed.

Sideslip. Patrollers also sideslip extensively in toboggan handling. Any slope too steep for the patroller to snowplow demands strong sideslip technique. You should be able to sideslip on steeper slopes both in deep heavy snow and on hard icy snow. Practice sideslipping on steep slopes for long distances, facing both directions. In deep snow it becomes more like sidestepping than sideslipping, but is often the only safe way to guide a loaded toboggan down a steep slope in deep snow.

After passing a volunteer ski patrol's ski test, you will become a "candidate." Candidates not already trained in first aid are given the National Ski Patrol's sixty-hour Winter Emergency Care Course before any on-hill training. Once ski season gets underway, the candidates are trained in toboggan handling, special on-the-hill first aid techniques, lift evacuation, and all the other aspects of patrolling. The training period is topped by practical and written tests before the candidates are allowed to wear the ski patrol coat and perform a patroller's duties.

If you ski at an area that depends on the services of volunteer ski patrollers and would like to join the patrol, talk to a patroller—they're friendly. Or, if you need to know what ski areas near you have volunteer patrols, contact the National Ski Patrol System, Inc., 133 South Van Gordon Street, Suite 100, Lakewood, CO 80228-1706.

Professional Ski Patrollers

If you've decided you want to become a professional patroller, you'll find that the road is a little longer than the volunteer route. Openings do exist, but finding the openings can be difficult.

Some resorts prefer to hire patrollers from within the company. That means you would have to work in another department of the resort until a ski patrol job became available. The employer's advantage in this arrangement is that the employer gets to see what kind of person you are before investing the considerable amount of time and training required to make you a professional ski patroller. Some advantages for you are: you get to see what kind of company you will be working for, what kind of housing is available, and other available benefits, such as summer job possibilities. Most ski areas give employees reduced-rate or even free skiing. If your skiing doesn't quite meet the requirements of the ski patrol you've chosen, working in another department at a ski area can give you the ski time you need to upgrade your skiing skills.

To find out if a ski area you are interested in hires from within or not, you'll need to write or travel to the areas you are interested in. *The White Book of Ski Areas* by Robert G. Enzel (Inter-Ski Services, Inc., P.O. Box 3635, Georgetown Station, Washington, DC 20007) lists the phone numbers and addresses of all the ski areas in the United States and Canada. Look for it in your library or bookstore. The book also lists whether a ski area uses pro or volunteer ski patrol. Also, *Ski Patrol Magazine,* published by the National Ski Patrol, sometimes has listings of ski areas with openings for professional patrollers.

As with volunteer patrols, spring is a good time to express your interest, fill out job applications, and have an informal ski test with the ski patrol director. August and September see many ski area personnel managers and patrol directors reviewing job applications and sending out job offers. Write or visit during those months, reminding the right people that you are still interested in the job. Besides expert ski ability, patrol directors look for previous first aid training and practical application of first aid (such as volunteer ambulance duty, lifeguard experience, or even Boy Scout experience), mountaineering or other outdoor experience, and a good attitude. A prospective employee with little experience but a good, positive attitude often stands a better chance of getting the job than someone with some experience but a poor attitude.

Physical Stamina

Ski patrolling can be hard physical work. In addition to the conditioning required of any active expert skier, pulling loaded toboggans demands extra endurance and strength. So does lifting injured skiers into toboggans, onto stretchers, and into vehicles. In the course of a day of ski patrolling, you may need to shovel out an entryway or stairway, pull on one end of a bogged down snowmobile until it is free, handle toboggans and lift injured skiers, and ski almost as many runs as a recreational skier.

Bicycling, running, and almost any sport you enjoy and participate in intensively will contribute to your overall fitness level. Bicycling is especially good conditioning for skiing, as it improves aerobic conditioning, leg strength, and knee flexibility. Younger skiers may not notice the need to maintain their knee flexibility or overall fitness, but I have found bicycling invaluable for maintaining my fitness level (which I once took for granted).

An hour of bicycling three or four times a week with plenty of uphill work is an excellent way to prepare for the ski season. Riding mountain bikes on trails adds a workout for your coordination and agility. For wintertime maintenance of your aerobic conditioning and knee flexibility, an indoor bike trainer is a good addition to your toy box. The bike trainer is basically a stand that supports your bike, with a fan or rollers for providing resistance to the back wheel. I can put in half an hour of bike training while watching the news on TV and feel I've hardly spent any time training.

Mountain bikes allow you to ride almost anywhere. Gravel roads and trails make an ideal, traffic-free training ground. *Karen Commins photo.*

For further leg strength work and for upper body conditioning, I use a portable stretch cord at home. The stretch cord is a long piece of latex tubing with a handle at either end and a device for attaching the middle of the cord to a door jamb. The cord provides a varied workout almost equal to one in a fully equipped gym. The cords are available from some mail-order houses and sporting goods stores.

I live in a rural area, and there is a health club with some weight training equipment in a nearby town. For my own purposes, I find it too time-consuming. A structured program, however, at a health club, gym, or YMCA does offer the advantage of expert advice and instruction, on equipment few people can keep at home. Also, when you've paid to use a club or gym, you may be more inclined to stick with your fitness program. As for me, I haven't paid any money, and laziness sometimes lets me shrug off a workout.

It's also possible to maintain a strength training program at home with little or no special equipment. Chin-ups on a homemade chin-up bar, one-third knee bends for leg strength, and perhaps some sets of push-ups are better than no training program. For further reading on fitness training, see the reading list at the end of this book.

Equipment

Along with expert skiing skills and fitness, both volunteer and professional ski patrollers need top-quality ski equipment and clothing. The rigors of patrolling leave no room for uncomfortable boots, malfunctioning bindings, fogged goggles, or wet clothing. In one season, a full-time professional patroller will ski more

SKI PATROLLER

days than the average recreational skier skis in five years. As a result, a patroller's equipment wears out much faster than most recreational skiers' equipment.

Many equipment and clothing manufacturers offer reduced prices to both professional and volunteer ski patrollers. Some of the programs are arranged through area representatives by mail order, while others are arranged through local ski shops. Many ski shops in ski country also offer discounts to patrollers for products not discounted by the manufacturer. While there have been complaints of abuse, this arrangement is still widespread. The shops and equipment manufacturers get free publicity, both through word of mouth and through the use of their products by ski patrollers. In this manner patrollers get much-appreciated help in obtaining the equipment they need.

Boots.

Boots are the most important part of a patroller's equipment. The long hours patrollers spend in their boots bring out quirks in feet and boots that the recreational skier might never notice. Different brands fit different types of feet, so just because a friend raves about his brand of boots you shouldn't decide that's the brand for you. Although a good fit is the most critical point in your choice of ski boots, you should also look for the control and support found in good-quality boots designed for advanced to expert skiers.

Try on as many different brands as you can when shopping for boots unless you are already sure one model fits you well. When trying on new boots, walk around the shop in them for a while and flex forward in them repeatedly. New boots will stretch slightly after some use, so a boot that is *very* comfortable in the shop may be too large. Be sure the shop you buy from can help you with fit problems that may arise later in the season — a good ski shop with knowledgeable employees is your best source when you're shopping for ski boots, and most patroller discounts on boots are arranged through ski shops.

If you have older boots you just can't part with, check them for compatibility with your bindings. Old, well broken-in boots are great and offer the ultimate in comfort, but some older models are incompatible with newer bindings. Also, worn heels and toes on boots can impair the binding function. If in doubt, ask a reputable ski shop.

Bindings.

Bindings are another vital part of your equipment and should be of recent vintage. Outdated bindings expose you to an unnecessary risk of injury, and they can also endanger those you are supposed to help. A worn-out binding may fail at any time. When rushing to put your skis on for an accident call, the last thing you need is a binding that fails to hold your boot, and sideslipping in front of a loaded toboggan is no place for a binding prone to unwanted releases.

Step-in bindings make the most sense for ski patrol work. As a patroller you may be in and out of your bindings a dozen times a day, and many of those times you need to be in or out in a hurry. All the major binding manufacturers make step-in bindings. If you are unsure about the suitability of an older binding, ask at a reputable ski shop.

The extra time you spend getting a good fit in ski boots will make a difference in your work.

Skis.   One pair of skis suited to the area you will patrol is enough to start patrolling. If you ski an area often, you probably already know what conditions prevail and what type of ski you like for those conditions. If you are new to the area, ask around at ski shops or ask other patrollers.

You may eventually want more than one pair of skis for varying conditions, or just for variety. First on your list should be a pair of "rock skis." The skiing public can choose where and when they ski—as a patroller, you can't. Early season conditions invariably include rocky skiing, especially for ski patrollers. If you don't own an old pair of skis you can use for rock skis, your first season as a patroller might turn your good skis into rock skis. Stringing boundary ropes before the ski area opens, marking rocky spots on the slopes, and, in the west, performing early-season avalanche control all expose your skis to incredible abuse. In a poor snow year, some patrollers go through two or three pairs of rock skis.

On a 1987 professional exchange at Big Sky, Montana, I didn't bring my rock skis even though I'd been warned to. I was following patroller Doug Kremer to an avalanche control route when we came to a long expanse of bare rock talus. Doug kept going across the rocks with his skis on. I hesitated, then followed. I muttered to myself, "Another spot like this, and I'm taking my skis off."

The next spot came soon enough, and there were four more bare patches after it. Doug never even slowed down. Not wanting to fall behind, I didn't take my skis off either. I couldn't believe I was doing this to my favorite cruising skis. Now I have two pairs of rock skis.

Yard sales in ski country and ski swaps are good sources of rock skis. Ski shops sometimes sell used "demo" and rental skis at good prices. I like older models of relatively high-performance skis, because I want a ski that will perform even if I am skiing on rocks. My personal favorites are the Dynastar MV2. They are an old giant slalom racing ski with a tough black base. The edges are an integral part of an inner metal layer, and in years of skiing on rocks I haven't torn out or even bent an edge.

Good rock skis rarely come with good bindings, if they come with bindings at all. I recommend putting good bindings on your rock skis—skiing on outdated bindings isn't worth the risk involved. If you own only one good pair of bindings, have a ski shop mount your good bindings on your rock skis and fill the old holes, or you can fill the holes yourself with epoxy glue. When snow covers the rocks, have the shop take the bindings off the rock skis and put them back on your good skis.

Poles.
Like skis, poles take a beating under the conditions of ski patrolling. Of course, patrollers like strong, light poles—the most expensive kind. Performance is only part of the reason patrollers favor the best poles. Poles made of soft aluminum bend and dent easily, and knocking ice off signs, ropes, and bamboo will quickly ruin a cheap ski pole. So, like much of a patroller's equipment, top-of-the-line poles work best in the long run.

Gloves.
Happily, gloves or mittens are one item you don't need to spend a lot of money on to get good use. Ski gloves are expensive; yet they wear out quickly when used for carrying signs, guiding toboggans, shoveling snow, and all

the other work a patroller routinely performs outside in the winter. I do own a pair of ski gloves, but I save them for the coldest days and use a more durable pair as much as possible.

My everyday work gloves for patrolling are oversized elkhide gloves from the local hardware store. (Elkhide mittens are also available.) I treat the gloves with a silicone/wax waterproofer and wear them over Army surplus wool glove liners. You can also use wool mittens under elkhide mittens, or polypropylene glove or mitten liners. The elkhide gloves cost about one-quarter what a pair of ski gloves costs, and they are quite warm. They far outlast conventional ski gloves or mittens.

Clothing.   Your choice of ski clothing depends largely on individual preference and the climate where you will patrol, but a few basics can help you stay comfortable in a wide range of conditions.

Layering is a simple principle. You stay warmer and can adapt to changing temperatures more easily in several light layers rather than one or two heavy ones. Light layers also wick away body moisture more easily than heavy ones. A light nylon wind shirt can do wonders when worn between a sweater and your turtleneck or other underwear. A wind shirt may be all you need to warm up on a day when you feel you haven't dressed quite warmly enough for the conditions.

Polypropylene, a man-made fiber, has all but replaced cotton for winter underwear. "Polypro" is an excellent insulating material, as the fibers can't absorb moisture. Polypro wicks body moisture away from the skin, giving a dry, comfortable feeling even after heavy exertion in wet weather. Manufacturers offer a colorful variety of sweaters made from polypropylene, and polypro bonded to a nylon shell makes an excellent coat. Polypro is also used in gloves, ski socks, turtlenecks, and ski hats.

Almost any ski pants will do if the area where you will patrol has liberal uniform requirements. Generally, though, area managements frown on baggy wool pants and jeans. Jeans aren't suitable for skiing anyway, unless you wear them under a pair of full-zip "warm-ups" or shells. Uninsulated zip-on pants can be versatile. The best ones are made of durable, water-resistant materials and have built-in snow cuffs. They can be worn over varying weights of long underwear, or over stretch pants on cold mornings when the weather is likely to warm up.

Stretch pants look good and are ideal for warm-weather spring skiing. For long-lasting stretch pants look for a pair made with a high wool content – 25 percent or more. I recommend a dark color – dark colors show dirt less easily than bright colors.

Skin Protection.   You may think that a deep mountain tan is the best way to attract members of the opposite sex, and perhaps it still is. But the harmful effects of sunlight are extreme at high altitudes, and by reflecting sunlight, snow intensifies the harmful effects. I use a number 15 sunblock every day of the ski season, and I recommend that any new patroller do the same. Being

outdoors every day will give you your tan quickly enough even through a 15 sunblock. If you have fair skin, consider using a lotion even stronger than 15, and limit your time in the sun whenever possible. In warm weather, don't forget to put lotion on the tops of your ears. I also recommend wearing a baseball cap in warm weather to keep the sun off your forehead and scalp.

Lips have none of the pigments that help your skin protect itself from the sun. Lips burn painfully if not protected by a sunblock lip protectant. I use a 15 sunblock lip protectant constantly in the winter to prevent cracking or chapping, and to limit the cumulative effects of the sun.

Protecting your eyes from high-altitude winter sunlight is even more important than protecting your skin. Long-term exposure to ultraviolet rays can permanently damage your eyesight, and going unprotected even one sunny day on the snow can sunburn your eyes – a painful condition that you can easily avoid by wearing goggles or sunglasses.

Sunglasses work well in fair weather, but good-quality goggles are a must for any ski patroller. Stormy days demand goggles that won't fog. On cold sunny days you need protection from the sun's ultraviolet rays and the rush of cold air created when you ski down the mountain.

On foggy days, you need to see as well as the conditions allow, so your goggles must be in good condition. The lenses should be relatively free of scratches. Most goggle manufacturers sell replacement lenses for their goggles, and badly scratched lenses should be replaced. The foam that seals the goggles around your face should be in good condition and be firmly attached to the goggles. If there are holes in the foam, the goggles should be replaced. Keeping your goggles free of moisture on the inside of the lens will help prevent moisture buildup.

Taking your goggles off your face and putting them on top of your head as you ride the lift guarantees that the goggles will fog when you put them back on. Perhaps it's because the goggles cool off while on top of your head (which is insulated by your hat) and heat up when you put them on, causing moisture to condense on the lens. Also, on a snowy day your hat may hold a surprising amount of moisture even if it feels dry. Then the moisture gets inside the goggles while they sit on your hat. Keeping your goggles on your face while riding the lift will help keep them fog-free.

———————◆———————

Ski patrol techniques and equipment change over the years, along with skiing's techniques and equipment. The first ski patrols in the United States bought wooden toboggans from the local hardware store, added some first aid supplies and blankets, and took to the slopes. The toboggans had no handles. One patroller in front straddled the toboggan, and another in the rear held onto a rope attached to the toboggan. For extra braking, they would tie a handful of rocks inside a triangular bandage and tie the bandage under the front of the toboggan. Somewhere along the way a patroller thought of putting metal handles on the front of a toboggan, and the all-fiberglass rescue toboggan wasn't far behind.

Advances in medicine, transportation, and ski patrolling all contribute to the high standard of care now available to skiers at developed ski areas. Today's ski patrols use much of the same equipment found on ambulances, and many patrollers serve on ambulances as Emergency Medical Technicians, or EMTs. EMT is the highest level of first aid training available in the United States. Ski areas and ski towns have medical clinics or hospitals, and an injured skier is usually only minutes, rather than hours, from a doctor's care. Severe cases are evacuated by helicopters manned by emergency room nurses or EMTs. The injuries that caused Frank Edson's death in 1936 might not be fatal today.

3

Handling Accidents

A school gym buzzes with activity. It looks like the aftermath of a disaster. One patient wears a head bandage. He has one arm in a sling and the other arm wrapped with gauze halfway to his elbow. A group of people in the corner are taking each other's blood pressure. Half a dozen people lie on the floor while others gather around and tie them onto backboards or put various types of splints on arms, legs, shoulders, and necks. It's not a disaster, though. It's the annual first aid refresher for a typical ski patrol.

Each fall thousands of ski patrollers across the United States and Canada participate in first aid refreshers. Every ski patroller must brush up on first aid skills regularly – we all tend to forget skills we don't often use. The refresher takes up a full weekend or more, because first aid, cardiopulmonary resuscitation, and on-the-hill skills all need attention before the ski season begins.

When a ski patroller helps an injured skier, he accepts a big responsibility. For example, when a skier has a suspected neck or back injury, the patroller at the skier's head is in charge and must keep the neck aligned while the other patrollers apply the cervical (neck) collar and strap the patient to a backboard. One false move could paralyze the patient for life. When I practice backboard techniques, I always hope that we won't have to use the techniques on the mountain. Yet we invariably end up tying several skiers to backboards each year. Most of the injuries turn out to be bruises or muscle strains, but occasionally a skier will fracture a vertebra and be in real danger of paralysis. The patroller can never know until a doctor examines the patient and the x-ray films.

Cardiopulmonary resuscitation (CPR) is another skill patrollers practice frequently yet hope they won't need. The cardiac arrest (heart attack) victim will die if you don't do something. He may die even if you do everything you possibly can.

Some people go through all the training required of a beginning patroller only to discover they dislike being around people who are actually hurt. The practice situations in first aid training often don't convey the reality of working with injured people. The first aid situations faced daily by patrollers range from minor injuries requiring simple commonsense treatment to serious accidents that tax the skills of experienced EMTs.

As a potential patroller, you would do well to examine your feelings. When you were a child and your little brother or your friend got hurt, did you want to help or did you feel like getting sick? Do you feel faint at the sight of other people's blood? If you've never been in such a situation, try to imagine how you would feel in charge of a seriously injured person. Serious accidents inevitably produce some tension among the patrollers involved, and a certain amount of tension is preferable to complacency. On the other hand, if you feel like the character in "M.A.S.H" who would love being a doctor "if only I didn't have to be around all those sick people all the time," then ski patrol work might not be for you.

For years the basic level of first aid training for ski patrollers was the American Red Cross Advanced First Aid Course. With Advanced First Aid and a CPR course, you would have been eligible to begin patrolling on just about any ski patrol in the United States. However, in 1987 the National Ski Patrol adopted a

Foreground: a pre-cut cardboard leg splint. Background: a quick splint.

SKI PATROLLER

new, higher level of training called the Winter Emergency Care course (WEC). The WEC provides first aid training that is designed specifically for ski patrollers and is more advanced in its techniques and terminology than the American Red Cross Advanced First Aid. Most ski patrols now require either WEC or EMT certification, although possessing a current Advanced First Aid card can make getting a WEC card easier.

Emergency Medical Technician, or EMT, is the most advanced level of first aid training available to the would-be patroller. EMT training is required of ambulance attendants, and most fire and police departments encourage their people to acquire EMT training. The course is usually offered by hospitals and prepares you to deal with a wide range of medical emergencies. The course can take up to six months. After completing the formal part of the instruction you'll be asked to perform ambulance duty as part of the course. Some professional patrols pay higher wages to patrollers with EMT certification.

Ski patrols affiliated with the National Ski Patrol offer WEC courses; as of this writing only those ski patrols have the instructors and course materials for WEC. The courses are usually offered in the fall of the year. Contact your local ski patrol or the National Ski Patrol for more information on WEC courses in your area. American Red Cross Advanced First Aid courses are available in many communities. For information on Red Cross courses, contact your local American Red Cross chapter.

A WEC or EMT course will acquaint you with a wide variety of first aid materials and equipment. Individual ski patrols use various types of equipment according to available funds, patrollers' preferences, and local or regional practices. The following are some commonly used materials and equipment.

Splints and Splinting Materials

Cardboard.   Cardboard is a versatile splinting material – with cardboard, a stapler, tape, and foam padding, you can make a splint for almost any situation. Once folded into a channel shape, as around an arm or leg, cardboard becomes quite rigid. I've even made a cardboard splint for a dislocated shoulder in a practice session, although I'd hate to take that much time with a real dislocated shoulder. For arms and legs, though, cardboard makes an excellent splint. Cardboard and foam padding (carpet pad scraps work well) are standard items for most toboggan packs. Pre-cut and pre-creased cardboard leg splints are available, and they're useful when a patient is going to a distant hospital. Often you can remove the quick splint or inflatable splint in the first aid room and apply a cardboard splint.

Quick Splint.   Also called the jiffy splint or box splint, the quick splint is widely used by ski patrols for leg injuries. It is easy to apply and inexpensive to build. It sandwiches the leg between two pieces of foam-padded plywood, and four or five straps with buckles hold the splint in place.

A wing splint. The cravat looped under the injured arm and tied over the opposite shoulder is key to holding the wing splint in place.

Wing Splint. The wing splint is used for splinting dislocated shoulders. It consists of two hinged rectangular pieces of plywood, each about two feet long and six inches wide. A third piece of wood hinged at both ends and slotted to accept a small bolt and wing nut holds the plywood in position. The wing splint is tied in position with cravats (triangular bandages folded into two-inch-wide strips).

Inflatable Splint. Also called an air splint, an inflatable splint is a vinyl or coated nylon bag, shaped somewhat like a leg with a zipper up the front. The simpler models have a valve much like those found on air mattresses, while the more elaborate ones have a special regulating valve that eliminates variations in inflation pressure due to changes in altitude or temperature. Air splints are easy to apply and will put a slight amount of traction on a fractured leg. This traction can be helpful.

Vacuum Splint. The vacuum splint consists of an airtight coated nylon bag filled with small Styrofoam beads. A tire valve keeps the vacuum in; a special pump is used to create the vacuum inside the splint. The force of the outside atmosphere on the foam beads causes the splint to become rigid. The advantage of the vacuum splint is that it conforms well to any body shape. As a result, it is ideal for dislocations of the shoulder, knee, or elbow.

Traction Splints. Traction splints are used for fractures of the femur— but only if the middle part of the femur is fractured. Suspected femur fractures near the hip joint or directly above the knee should not be splinted with traction.

Several types of traction splints are in use today. The simplest is the Thomas half-ring. With the half-ring, cravats are used to hold the leg in position and also to provide the traction. Two improvements on the half-ring are the Hare traction splint and the Sager traction splint. The Sager is the newer one of the two and offers the advantage of a spring-loaded system with a scale that shows the amount of traction being applied.

Backboards. A backboard is in effect a splint for the entire body. Its purpose is to hold the spine in a stable position without any possible movement.

A vacuum splint as it would be used to support a dislocated shoulder. The vacuum is created using the pump in the model's right hand.

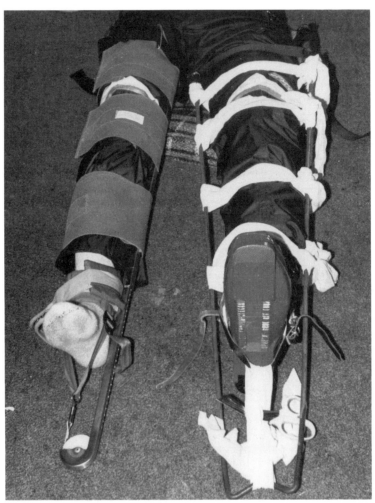

Left: Sager traction splint. Right: Thomas half-ring.

Backboards are also useful for transporting people with hip, pelvis, and upper femur injuries. A backboard is usually made of thick plywood with stiffeners added.

Personal Equipment

In addition to all the equipment carried on toboggans or kept ready at summit stations, every patroller carries an assortment of supplies and equipment in a fanny pack or vest. Your personal first aid pack's contents will depend on your

SKI PATROLLER

preference and on local requirements. A bare minimum for any first aid pack includes the following: two or three triangular bandages, two or three roller bandages (roller gauze), several sterile gauze pads, a roll of adhesive tape, adhesive bandages (Band-Aid, Curad, and so forth), scissors (lightweight all-purpose "EMT" type), CPR mask with one-way valve, vinyl examination gloves, short pencil, accident report form, and a kitchen-size plastic garbage bag. I like to keep all the small items in the plastic bag, keeping the inside of my pack a little less cluttered. Optional items include, but are not limited to: Swiss Army knife or Leatherman all-purpose tool, space blanket, seam ripper, antiseptic swabs, whistle, and personal items such as sunblock, lip protectant, and the like.

Depending on your ski area's policy, you may also need to carry a lift self-evacuation kit consisting of one hundred feet or more of 5mm or 6mm climbing rope, a web sling, and locking carabiner. It's no wonder many patrollers now favor the patrol vest. Descended from the fishing vest, the patrol vest has zippered pockets on every square inch, including a large pocket in the rear for lift evacuation gear or other bulky items. The weight is distributed more evenly than with a fanny pack, and some models include a place for your radio and Pieps.

If you become a volunteer patroller, you'll probably be required to purchase a fanny pack or vest and the contents. The fanny pack is still the standard for many patrols, so check before purchasing a vest. The vest may not fit in with the area's uniforms. Fanny packs cost from twenty to forty dollars. Most professional patrols provide a fanny pack or vest and first aid supplies, but you will probably still have to buy your evacuation gear. The cost for evacuation gear in 1988 was thirty to forty dollars.

Toboggans

A descendant of the old hardware-store wooden toboggan is still in use today at a few ski areas. The modern version has long tubular aluminum handles rigidly attached to the front, aluminum tailfins underneath, a chain brake under the

A typical fanny pack and some of its contents. Note the CPR pocket mask in its plastic case on the right, and the vinyl exam gloves draped over the front flap.

The author models his patrol vest. Note the zipper for the rear pocket at lower right. *Scott Bohr photo.*

front, and a tailrope. Although heavier than the fiberglass Cascade common at many ski areas, the wood toboggan handles very well on a wide range of snow conditions. A stokes litter is attached to the toboggan and can be removed with the patient for transportation in vehicles. This type of toboggan has been in continuous use since the 1930s at Sun Valley, Idaho, and is often referred to as the Sun Valley toboggan. The toboggans are also manufactured under the brand name Todboggan.

The Cascade toboggan was invented in the Cascade Mountains of Washington State, and is constructed of molded fiberglass. It is widely used across the United States, and the Cascade Toboggan Company has grown to supply ski patrols with much of the specialized rescue equipment they need.

A ski patroller uses a Sun Valley toboggan on a foggy day at Sun Valley.

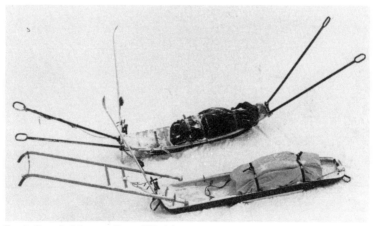

Front: Cascade toboggan. Rear: Akia toboggan.

The handles on a Cascade are attached with a removable pivot pin and removable handle locks. The handles can be used unlocked, so they can pivot up and down – or locked, so pressure can be put on the front of the toboggan to get more advantage from the brake chain. The handles can also be quickly removed, and a rope handle at each corner makes the toboggan easy to lift off the snow.

Like the Sun Valley type, Cascade toboggans have aluminum fins attached to the bottom to help provide stability. Nylon straps with quick release buckles help hold the patient in the toboggan.

The Akia and Crystal toboggans share the same basic design. The Akia is made in Austria of aluminum; the Crystal was invented at Washington's Crystal Mountain and is made of fiberglass. The Akia type is designed for two handlers. Instead of a tailrope on the rear, this type has a second set of handles that give the toboggan a double-ended appearance. In fact, except for the placement of the chain brake, the Akia and Crystal toboggans could be handled with either end forward. The two sets of handles also make it easy to pick the toboggans up while you're skiing – a useful feature in deep snow or long flat areas inaccessible by snowmobile. (Snowmobiles are commonly used to pull toboggans out of flat areas and up hills, but they are limited to packed snow.)

Toboggan Handling.   Skiing with an empty Cascade or Sun Valley toboggan is easy once you learn the basics. Ski normally, gripping the handles with your hands at your sides or slightly ahead of you. A Sun Valley type, with its long handles and wood body, is flexible enough to keep the tailfins in the snow under most conditions. An empty Cascade, however, can lose contact with the snow in the rear, where the tailfins are located. There are two schools of thought regarding this potential problem. The old school says you should ski the empty

A ski patroller approaches the scene of an accident with an empty Cascade toboggan.

Two patrollers negotiate a turn with an Akia toboggan.

Cascade with the handles unlocked, allowing them to change position with changes in the terrain. A newer school advocates skiing with the handles locked, whether empty or loaded. As with many of the techniques of ski patrolling, local preference and custom will dictate which method you use. Chain brakes on all types should be up and out of the snow when the toboggan is empty.

The Akia type, while designed for two handlers, can be skied empty by one. Since it has no fins, the Akia can be tricky on hard snow and you need to avoid quick turns. Staying directly down the fall line from the toboggan will help you avoid having the Akia pass you going down the hill. In soft snow, the empty Akia behaves much better, and its handling is similar to a Cascade with one handler.

If the empty toboggan (any type) does pass you and tries to pull you down the hill, it's not a hopeless situation. Above all, keep a firm grip on the handles. Switch hands on the handles as the toboggan passes you and keep a strong stance on your skis. You should be able to steer the toboggan ahead of you like a wheelbarrow. When you're ready, steer the toboggan until you're below it. Perform the maneuver in one smooth motion – if you hesitate while the toboggan is alongside you, it may get below you again. When you handle a toboggan, always keep a grip on the handles with at least one hand.

Handling an Akia with two operators is an exercise in teamwork. The front handler must tell the rear handler when he plans to turn, and the speed must be kept low during turns. If the front handler makes a turn too fast, the rear handler will get a whiplash effect that can throw him off balance, or at least force him to let go of the handles.

HANDLING ACCIDENTS

One patroller assesses an injury while another opens the toboggan pack.

When skiing any empty toboggan to an accident, you should ski as quickly but as safely as possible. Look ahead and pick your route when skiing with a toboggan, whether it's empty or loaded. Give skiers plenty of room when passing or approaching them, and ski defensively on crowded slopes. If a skier seems to be crossing in front of you or is otherwise unaware of your approach, yell "Ski patrol! Toboggan!" while preparing to stop or take evasive action.

As you approach the accident, slow down and decide which direction you will want the toboggan to face. The toboggan should always be parked across the fall line, so you should come in fairly far from the patient. The toboggan will make a shorter radius turn behind you, and you don't want it to hit the patient. If a patroller is already at the scene, he or she is in charge of the accident and may tell you how to bring in the toboggan.

Bring the toboggan in carefully below the injured person. If another patroller is already at the scene, he will help you and use his skis to secure the toboggan in place. If not, you will need to make sure the toboggan doesn't slide away while you remove your skis. Plant your skis tail first through the rope handles or alongside the toboggan on the downhill side to keep the toboggan in place.

SKI PATROLLER

After securing the toboggan, you can begin to assess the injured person's condition. If another patroller has already begun an assessment and doesn't need help immediately, you can unpack the pack contents and get the toboggan ready by arranging the pad and blankets. The toboggan pack generally contains blankets, a foam pad the length and width of the sled, and various splints and splinting materials. A heavy piece of nylon or canvas protects the pack's contents when the toboggan is empty. When you have a passenger, the cloth is unfolded and used to protect him.

How you act around the patient and how you communicate with him are very important. You should be calm and reassuring. Avoid making statements that might alarm the patient, such as "Boy, that looks bad." As you talk to the patient, try to find out how the accident happened, and avoid expressing your opinion as to why the accident may or may not have happened. Don't say, "That binding should have released" or "This bump shouldn't have been here." Keep your comments to the facts at hand. Do make a mental note, however, of any comments the injured person makes about the accident.

Once you have cared for the patient's injuries, you are ready to move him into the toboggan. Individual circumstances will dictate exactly how you get the patient into the toboggan. In many cases the injured person can help you. Repositioning the toboggan as close to the patient as possible is a useful move and may be necessary if the patient can't help. If the patient can't help and only two patrollers are at the scene, you may have to enlist the aid of some bystanders.

Bystanders at accidents often are friends or relatives of the injured person and are eager to help. If you do use bystanders' assistance, be sure to tell them exactly what you want them to do and when. If no bystanders are available, two patrollers can move a patient into the toboggan. One patroller kneels on one knee in the toboggan, with the toboggan between him and the patient. The other patroller kneels, also on one knee, on the other side of the patient.

One patroller slips his hands under the patient's shoulders and waist. The other patroller slips his hands under the patient's back and butt or thighs. When both patrollers are ready, they lift the patient and move him into the toboggan in one motion. The patient is lifted only as much as required to get him into the toboggan.

Whether you put the patient in the toboggan to ride with his head uphill or downhill depends on the nature of the injury. The rule of thumb is to have the injury uphill. Transporting a patient with a suspected leg fracture with the injury uphill accomplishes three things: you are elevating the injury (reducing blood flow to the injured limb, thereby reducing swelling and pain); you are treating the patient for shock (elevating the feet above the abdomen); and you are protecting the patient from further injury (riding down in the toboggan, the patient may slide toward the front of the toboggan – with the injured leg downhill, the patient's weight might bear down on the leg and cause more pain or even further injury). Some other general guidelines are: head downhill for shock, hypothermia, lower extremity injuries, abdominal injuries (unless the patient is short of breath); head uphill for head, neck, face, chest, and upper extremity injuries; also head uphill for shortness of breath and unconsciousness. Patients with chest

Snowplowing with a loaded toboggan.

wounds or multiple rib fractures should be positioned so they're lying on the injured side with the head uphill.*

When you secure the straps that hold the patient in the toboggan, be sure they are snug, but don't overtighten any that are directly over an injury. If possible, let the patient get his hands near his face before you secure the strap nearest the head. This gives a less claustrophobic feeling and lets the patient adjust the blankets and pack cover around his face if he wants. If the patient's hat has come off, replace it on his head if possible, and on snowy days you might replace goggles as well.

After securing the patient in the toboggan, you are ready to put your skis on. On steeper slopes, your partner will need to hold the toboggan while you get into your bindings. Then you can do the same while your partner gets into his bindings.

Local custom and the terrain will dictate whether your partner will assist you by hanging onto the tailrope. Some patrols require a tailrope handler on nearly all terrain; others let the patrollers decide if they need the tailrope. When you first start downhill with a Cascade on a steep slope, it is helpful to have your partner hold tension on the tailrope until you get the toboggan pointed downhill. This keeps the rear end of the toboggan from sliding sideways and offsets the Cas-

---

* Bowman, Warren, *Outdoor Emergency Care* (Denver: National Ski Patrol, 1988), 336–37. A later portion of this chapter discusses whether a skier with a heart condition should lie uphill or downhill on the toboggan.

cade's tendency to tip over as you pull the handles sideways into the fall line. On gentle slopes you can simply ski away.

Always keep the patient's comfort in mind when skiing with a loaded toboggan. Time is not as important as a safe and comfortable ride. Look ahead and pick your route well in advance, and try to stay in the fall line as much as possible.

On packed snow, your technique depends on the steepness of the slope. On gentle runs, you can snowplow down the fall line with the brake off. On slightly steeper runs, snowplow with the chain brake down. On the steepest runs, you will need to sideslip in front of the toboggan with the chain brake down. On steep icy slopes, you may want someone holding the tailrope for extra braking power.

Whenever I have a loaded toboggan in the powder, I look for the nearest packed run and try to get to it. Going down the fall line in deep powder with a toboggan is hard work—a sure way to work up a sweat on the coldest day. Snowplowing and sideslipping usually won't work. If the slope is gentle enough you can run straight down the fall line, but most runs steep enough for skiing on a powder day (and where skiers might get hurt) are too steep to allow straight running with the toboggan. Sidestepping is the only way down a steep fall line.

Sideslipping with a loaded toboggan.

Traversing with a loaded Cascade toboggan.

Getting to a packed run by the shortest route usually forces you to traverse. To traverse with a loaded Cascade or Sun Valley, push down on the uphill handle and pull up slightly on the downhill handle. This will cause the toboggan to ride a "platform" of snow in soft snow and cause the uphill fin to bite into packed snow. On all but the gentlest slopes you will need a second patroller to assist you. The second patroller takes hold of the tailrope, and staying well uphill and slightly ahead of the rear of the toboggan, keeps the rear from sliding downhill.

The tailrope handler can also help pull the toboggan forward if you bog down in a drift or take too high a traverse. It's better to take the high road around a tree and lose some momentum than go too fast below the tree. Remember that your tailrope handler must stay uphill of the toboggan. If you go too fast or cut too close to the downhill side of a tree you may force your tailrope handler to let go of the rope or run into the toboggan.

Traversing with an Akia or Crystal and two handlers is fairly simple. Both handlers pick up slightly on the handles, letting the toboggan ride on its uphill edge. Turning an Akia takes teamwork. The front handler calls out when he anticipates a turn, then starts a gradual turn. On steep terrain, a safer method is

SKI PATROLLER

To hold a high traverse or get across flat terrain, patrollers can pick up an Akia toboggan.

to stop while the rear handler holds the toboggan and the front handler makes a kick turn. Then the front handler holds the toboggan while the rear handler makes his kick turn. Two handlers can also sidestep or snowplow with the Akia anywhere the terrain calls for those methods.

If you fall while skiing with a loaded toboggan, don't let go of the handles. Anywhere but on the steepest, iciest slopes, the toboggan won't run over you or take off on its own. As long as you keep the toboggan above you and in the fall line, you should be able to stop the toboggan and retrieve your ski. The potential for such problems, however remote, is the reason some patrols require a tailrope handler on all toboggans.

As you work your way downhill, stop occasionally and ask the patient how he or she is doing. Ask if the ride is too fast or too rough, and slow down if the answer is yes. In serious injury cases, a patroller should stay close to the patient's head to monitor the patient's condition. Never leave any loaded toboggan unattended.

Special Toboggan Techniques. People with dislocated shoulders usually object to lying down. Even after splinting, a dislocated shoulder causes too much pain in a supine position. To allow the patient to ride comfortably sitting up, you need some kind of backrest. Some patrols put a specially made folding seatback in each toboggan. Otherwise a patroller must act as the backrest. To do this, the patient sits in the front half of the toboggan with his feet propped against the front of the toboggan. The patroller can either sit with his back against the patient's back or face the same direction as the patient with his legs on either side of the patient. Sitting back to back makes it easier for the patroller to support the patient's back, but sitting with the patroller's legs on either side is easier if the patient needs side support. Local custom will probably influence which method you use.

Another special technique you should know of enables ski patrollers to transport a cardiac arrest victim while maintaining CPR. More Americans die from heart attacks than from any other single cause. Statistics show that any American male over age 35 is a likely candidate for a heart attack, and the risk jumps dramatically for those over 40.

Arrhythmia, or abnormal rhythm, causes almost half of all heart attack fatalities, and CPR is effective in maintaining a regular pulse in a patient with arrhythmia. Effective CPR, promptly initiated, has the potential to save many lives, but CPR can't be interrupted for more than a few seconds if it is to remain effective. Patrollers can't maintain CPR indefinitely, but they must maintain effective CPR while transporting a heart attack victim off the mountain to where he can receive medical attention. Patrollers faced with this difficult situation have several choices. The area ski patrol decides which method to use.

One method that works in most situations is to place two toboggans side by side and tie, tape, or strap them together. Two persons can then perform the CPR. This method works especially well with Cascade toboggans, since the handles of two Cascades placed side by side line up exactly next to each other. Another method involves one toboggan, and one rescuer to do the CPR.

A patroller supports a dislocated shoulder patient for transport in a toboggan.

SKI PATROLLER

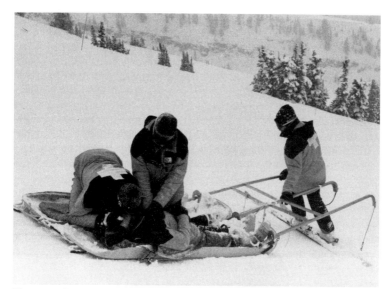

Three patrollers use two toboggans to maintain CPR while transporting a patient off the mountain.

To maintain CPR and transport the patient with the use of two toboggans, you need a minimum of three patrollers – two to perform CPR and one to handle the toboggans. On steeper slopes, a fourth patroller is needed to help with the toboggans by holding onto the tailrope.

Place the toboggans side by side facing the same direction. Tape the handles together with several wraps of first aid tape, once near the front of the handles and again near the base of the handles. Take one tailrope and make a couple of passes through the rope handles nearest each other at the rear of the sleds. Then tie two half hitches around the loops of rope between the two handles. Run the rest of that tailrope to the front of the toboggan and use it to tie the two front rope handles together. Wrap the other tailrope a couple of times around the tie-up at the rear so its pull will be evenly distributed.

Both toboggan pads should be placed in the toboggan that the rescuers will kneel in – CPR is more effective if the patient is on a hard surface, and the rescuers' knees will need the padding. Loosely buckle the straps in the rescuers' toboggan so the rescuers can use the straps for footholds. If enough help is available, two patrollers can get into position in the toboggan while one or two others maintain CPR. When all is ready, the patient is quickly transferred to the empty toboggan and CPR continues.

With one patroller on the front handles and another on the tailrope, the team is ready to start downhill. Depending on the steepness of the slope, one or both brake chains can be used.

For single-toboggan CPR, the patient is placed in the toboggan and a single rescuer straddles the patient. The rescuer must modify his hand position from the standard CPR position – the hands will be placed transversely to, or across, the patient's chest rather than parallel to the body as in normal CPR. The single-toboggan, single-rescuer method has the advantage of simplicity and maneuverability. On moguled slopes, in thick trees, or anywhere two toboggans would be impractical, the single-toboggan method would be best. On groomed slopes where maneuverability is not a problem, two toboggans and two rescuers give the advantage of two-rescuer CPR, which can be more effective than single-rescuer CPR and is less tiring for the rescuers. With either method, the toboggan handlers should go slowly to avoid upsetting the balance of the patrollers performing CPR.

A controversy exists within the ski patrol community as to whether a CPR patient's head should be uphill or downhill during transport in a toboggan. One theory holds that the patient's head should be uphill because it is much easier for the rescuers to maintain a stable position and therefore maintain effective CPR; the head-uphill position also reduces the patient's tendency to vomit, which complicates the transportation process. *Outdoor Emergency Care,* the WEC textbook, states that heart attack victims should be transported head uphill.

The other theory holds that the patient's head should be downhill because gravity will tend to pool the patient's blood in the head and chest where it is needed most. The rescuers' position should be considered secondary, goes the thinking, and the increased tendency to vomit is considered offset by gravity's help in removing the vomitus from the patient's mouth and airway. No medical studies have been made proving one position better than the other.

First Aid Room Procedures

Most resorts have either a first aid room or a medical clinic at the base area. If you're lucky enough to patrol at an area with a medical clinic, your work on an accident may end with the paperwork. If the ski area is located some distance from a hospital or medical clinic, you'll probably transfer the patient from the toboggan to a bed in the first aid room and continue caring for him.

Some first aid rooms have a ramp and a special door that allows bringing the loaded toboggan directly inside. Once inside, the toboggan rests on a platform at gurney height, bypassing the extra effort and risk involved in carrying a patient on a stretcher. If your first aid room isn't equipped with a toboggan door and ramp, you will need to transfer the patient first to a stretcher, then carry the patient inside, put the stretcher on a gurney, and finally transfer the patient to a bed.

Once inside, you can make the patient more comfortable and perform more detailed first aid measures than are practical on the hill. If you haven't already removed the patient's ski boots, arrival in the first aid room gives you the opportunity to remove the boots under ideal conditions. Most hospital personnel feel that patrollers are better qualified to remove ski boots than they are and prefer to have patients arrive in the hospital without their boots.

Toboggans enter the first aid room at Solitude Ski Area in Utah through this special door. Once inside, the toboggan is at gurney height. *Scott Bohr photo.*

Removing the boot from an injured leg is easiest with three patrollers, although two can manage it. In cold weather, a conventional four- or five-buckle boot remains cold and stiff even after being brought inside. A conventional boot will be easier to remove if you can allow it to warm up for a few minutes; rear entry boots come off fairly easily and don't need warming.

Start by removing the splint, if one has already been applied. (An exception is a traction splint—traction, once applied, should not be released except by a doctor.) Leaving the splint under the injured leg makes reapplication of the splint

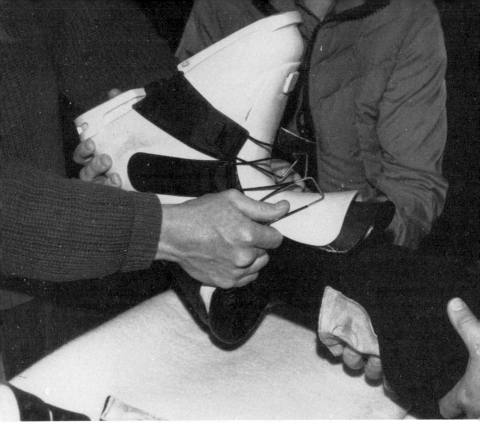

Removing the ski boot from an injured leg.

easier once the boot is off. Next carefully loosen the boot as much as possible. Be certain that all buckles are completely unbuckled, and that any hook-and-pile straps on the liners are undone.

One or two patrollers then stand or kneel at the patient's feet, and a third is at the side nearest the injured leg. The patroller at the side lifts the leg slightly. If the patient's pants are loose enough, use the "pantleg pinch lift": Pinch or roll the extra pantleg material; then pick up the leg by holding the pantleg. One hand should be placed above the injury and one hand below it (that is, one hand *distal* – below the injury – and the other hand *proximal* – higher up on the leg than the injury itself). If the pants are too tight for this method, the patroller lifting the leg should gently grasp the leg above and below the injury and lift.

Another patroller then slides his hands down inside the boot on either side of the ankle. This patroller steadies the ankle while the third patroller spreads the boot open, pulls the tongue out, and carefully rotates the boot off the heel, then slides it upward off the toes. If only two patrollers are present, one lifts the leg and steadies the injury while the other spreads the boot and gently rotates it off.

SKI PATROLLER

The method can be changed slightly according to the type of injury. A boot-top fracture demands very gentle handling, and the patroller who steadies the ankle, instead of using the "pantleg pinch lift," should steady the leg above and below the injury, at the ankle, and just above the boot top. Sprained knees normally aren't as touchy as fractures, and the boot can easily be removed by one or two patrollers.

Follow-up

Once you have finished all possible first aid measures, including recording pulse and blood pressure when indicated, it's time to start your paperwork. Accurate accident reports are important for several reasons. With today's legal climate, accurate accident reports help protect the ski area and its insurance company in case an injured person later sues the ski area for damages. Accurate reporting also helps the ski industry compile statistics that can point out trends in skier injuries. These statistics help with ski binding research and development, and skier safety programs. When reports tell exactly where accidents have occurred, area management may be able to identify problem traffic areas that need better signing, grooming, or summer trail work.

Most serious accidents require extra paperwork covering accident investigations. Even minor injuries – if they occur on skis rented from the ski area, or while the injured person is loading or unloading from a lift – usually require extra paperwork from the departments involved. At small areas the ski patrol director usually handles accident investigations, while larger resorts use teams of supervisors or full-time risk managers who take care of accident follow-up.

As soon as you or your partner begins the paperwork for an accident, the other should prepare the toboggan for its return to service. At small ski areas, it's important to return the toboggan to the mountain promptly. Accidents seem to come in waves – one day you might see few or no accidents, and the next day might be a "wreck-o-rama." When accidents come one after another at a small ski area, the most pressing problem besides having enough patrollers to go around is making toboggans available.

Returning a toboggan to the mountain usually involves carrying the toboggan up a lift. For chairlifts, most ski areas use a carrier that hangs the toboggan from the chair. The carrier clips onto eyebolts on the toboggan or the wire litter on a Sun Valley type, and makes it possible to load and unload the toboggan without stopping the lift. Loading is easier if the lift is slowed down, however, and a lift operator or another patroller can help get the toboggan and carrier in position as the chair approaches.

When unloading with center-post chairs, be sure you hold the carrier from in front of the chair post. Holding on from behind the post will cause you to get caught on the chair, carried around the bullwheel, and perhaps injured. Hold the toboggan carrier with one hand and push away from the chair with the other hand as soon as the toboggan is fully on the unloading ramp and before you reach the part of the ramp that descends below the chair. Once you are off the lift and out of the way of skiers, you can send the carrier back down on the lift.

A patroller transports a toboggan up the lift on a snowy morning.

Areas that don't use carriers on their chair lifts may use several alternative methods for transporting toboggans up the lift. One way is to tie the tailrope to the front of the toboggan, forming a loop over the toboggan that is placed over the back of the chair. The rope is tied short enough so the toboggan just clears the ramp.

Toboggans without tailropes, such as Akias or Crystals, can be held on the patroller's lap. The handles must be removed and strapped to the toboggan, or they might strike lift towers and knock the toboggan out of the patroller's hands. Carrying the toboggan on your lap has the advantage of allowing the lift to keep running as you load, but it can be uncomfortable on long lifts and it causes wear and tear on your ski clothing.

A toboggan can also be tied or wedged crosswise onto a chair by itself, with the patroller in the chair ahead. When the patroller reaches the top of the lift, he signals the lift operator to stop the lift and unloads the toboggan. Handles on all

SKI PATROLLER

types of toboggans should be removed or folded back and tied to the toboggan with this method.

With the toboggan back at its station, you have completed the cycle of accident and toboggan handling. Rescuing an injured skier takes skill, and as with any skill, the feeling of having performed well is its own reward. But knowing you've rescued an injured skier and prevented further injury is particularly satisfying.

Sometimes you'll get a thank-you note. At other times a skier you've rescued will express hearty thanks in person. That's like icing on the cake. The cards, letters, and thank-yous keep many patrollers coming back year after year, even when their knees or their spouses tell them they've been patrolling too long.

4

Safety Principles and Skier Education

The noise level builds on the college ski bus as it approaches the ski area parking lot. Everyone on board is eager to go skiing. The sun is out and new snow covers the trees along the road. As the bus pulls to a stop and everyone starts to get up, the door opens and two ski patrollers jump on. After getting the attention of the students, they introduce themselves and begin detailing the safety rules of the ski area.

"We have slow skiing areas around the mountain," says Frank. "They are marked with orange and black 'Slow' or 'Slow Skiing' banners and signs. Those signs mean exactly what they say. If we catch someone skiing fast in those areas, we will mark that skier's ticket and remind him to ski slower. The second time, we'll take away the lift ticket and the individual will be done skiing for the day."

"The same goes for our 'No Jumping' signs," adds Jim. "They are posted at various places around the mountain where jumping is not allowed. Now, we all like to catch a little air now and then, and parts of the mountain are open for jumping. But any people jumping at places posted 'No Jumping' will get their tickets marked and will get a safety talk from us. The second time we will take your lift ticket, and you'll be done skiing for the day.

"The same ticket marking policy goes for reckless skiing anywhere on the mountain. If a patroller sees you skiing recklessly, such as going too fast on crowded runs, causing collisions or near collisions, jumping onto groomed runs from the sides, or doing anything else a patroller thinks is reckless, the patroller will stop you, give you a safety talk, and mark your ticket. Anyone with a marked ticket who is stopped by a patroller for any reason will lose his or her lift ticket."

"You've probably heard of the six rules of the Skier's Responsibility Code," says Frank. "The first rule says you should ski in control and in such a manner that you can stop or avoid other skiers or objects. It's the most important rule in skiing, and we hope you all ski by it. Thanks for your time, and have fun."

A patroller reminds a busload of college students to ski safely.

Reducing the Dangers

Accident prevention is a major goal of every ski patrol and should be for every ski patroller. Accident prevention measures range from simple acts like marking exposed rocks or stumps to more active efforts like educating skiers. Marking hazards and placing warning signs are everyday chores for patrollers, and while skier education gives less obvious results, the benefits last longer. A skier who is aware of safety when he skis is less likely to need signs, bamboos, and the other markings to avoid injury. An educated skier tends to ski in control and watch for potential hazards, instead of depending on the ski patrol to eliminate the risks involved in skiing.

An educated skier also tends to realize that some risks remain in the sport of skiing no matter what, and that ski areas cannot be held responsible every time

SKI PATROLLER

someone is injured. The liability insurance costs of ski areas have skyrocketed because of a few huge court settlements and a growing number of "nuisance" suits – lawsuits brought against ski areas by persons who were injured through no fault of the ski area in hope that the area will settle out of court.

Safety awareness among skiers, with the theme of skiing in control, is the focus of a major skier education program sponsored by the ski industry. Using modern ski equipment on today's groomed runs, even an advanced intermediate skier can reach speeds of thirty or forty miles an hour. Improved grooming and ski equipment have contributed to a decline in the total number of ski injuries, but the number of serious and fatal accidents has grown slightly. Typically, in fatal cases, a male skier in his mid-twenties hits a tree at high speed and sustains fatal head or chest injuries. Although the ratio of deaths to skier visits is low compared to other risky sports (.45 deaths per 100,000 skier visits, 2 deaths per 100,000 football participant days, and 2.8 deaths per 100,000 participant days for water sports), educating younger skiers appears to be a useful way to reduce the number of skiing deaths.* The number of less serious accidents can also be reduced by skier education.

As the sport of skiing has grown, so has the ski patrol's role in making skiing a safer sport. From its beginning in 1938, the National Ski Patrol has published booklets and articles aimed at making skiers aware of safe skiing principles. In 1936, before he organized the National Ski Patrol, Minnie Dole published a ski safety report in the American Ski Annual that identified causes of accidents and ways to prevent them. Since then, the causes and the suggested prevention measures have changed remarkably little. Dole's report stated that skiers got hurt by going too fast for conditions, and suggested that "clubs and instructors emphasize the fact that it is disgraceful to ski out of control habitually."**

Today the National Ski Patrol works closely with the National Ski Areas Association (NSAA) and other ski industry organizations to produce training materials and seminars for patrollers. The National Ski Patrol and National Ski Areas Association also cooperate to produce videos, posters, magazine ads, and other skiing safety materials addressed to the skiing public, and several videotapes are available that get various ski safety messages across in an entertaining way.

When patrollers visit schools, ski clubs, or other groups, the visit can be easily organized around a showing of the videos, and some ski areas use the films as a way to educate skiers who have been stopped by the ski patrol for skiing recklessly. The skiers are given the choice of watching the video or losing their lift ticket for the day. Most choose to watch the video.

The videos "Tony's Flight" and "Ski Sense and Safety" are excellent tools for patrols to use in their skier education efforts. "Tony's Flight," produced by NSAA, documents the death of a young ski racer named Tony, who was skiing at high

---

* Shealy, Jasper E., "How Dangerous Is Skiing and Who's at Risk?" *Ski Patrol Magazine,* Winter 1986, 21.

** Besser, Gretchen R., *The Natural Ski Patrol: Samaritans of the Snow* (Woodstock, Vt.: The Countryman Press, 1983), 27.

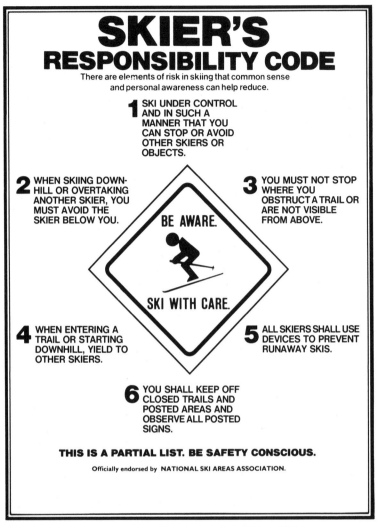

SKIER'S
RESPONSIBILITY CODE

There are elements of risk in skiing that common sense
and personal awareness can help reduce.

1 SKI UNDER CONTROL
AND IN SUCH A
MANNER THAT YOU
CAN STOP OR AVOID
OTHER SKIERS OR
OBJECTS.

2 WHEN SKIING DOWN-
HILL OR OVERTAKING
ANOTHER SKIER, YOU
MUST AVOID THE
SKIER BELOW YOU.

3 YOU MUST NOT STOP
WHERE YOU
OBSTRUCT A TRAIL OR
ARE NOT VISIBLE
FROM ABOVE.

BE AWARE.

SKI WITH CARE.

4 WHEN ENTERING A
TRAIL OR STARTING
DOWNHILL, YIELD TO
OTHER SKIERS.

5 ALL SKIERS SHALL USE
DEVICES TO PREVENT
RUNAWAY SKIS.

6 YOU SHALL KEEP OFF
CLOSED TRAILS AND
POSTED AREAS AND
OBSERVE ALL POSTED
SIGNS.

THIS IS A PARTIAL LIST. BE SAFETY CONSCIOUS.

Officially endorsed by **NATIONAL SKI AREAS ASSOCIATION.**

This is one of many posters available to ski areas from National Ski Areas
Association.

speed after a race when another skier skied in front of him. Skiing too fast to
stop, Tony missed the skier but crashed into a group of trees and was fatally
injured. "Tony's Flight" includes interviews with Tony's parents and friends, and is
a moving account that points out the dangers even expert skiers court when
skiing fast on public ski runs. The video is ideal for high school and college
groups – they are the ones most likely to ski faster than their ability warrants, and
Tony was in high school at the time of his death.

"Ski Sense and Safety," produced by Mammoth Mountain Ski Area in California, emphasizes the rules of safe skiing as they are summarized in the Skier's Responsibility Code. A cartoon character named Mogul Mike leads viewers through the Skier's Responsibility Code in an entertaining way, and the film also features real-life Olympic Silver Medalist Christin Cooper.

Visiting schools during ski season is an excellent way for patrollers to reach young skiers. If the school has a skiing program, as many schools in snow country do, the visit can be timed to come just before the students' first on-the-hill session. If the school doesn't have a skiing program but does have a ski club or collegiate racing program, arrangements can be made to meet with those groups.

Patrollers might start a typical talk by introducing themselves, and if the group is young, one patroller might ask if anyone knows what the ski patrol does. Many middle school and high school students think the ski patrol's only job is to take away fast skiers' tickets—or just "to ski." Other ways to make the talks interesting include demonstrating how a toboggan works, or bringing in mountain signs and explaining what they mean.

After showing "Tony's Flight" or "Ski Sense and Safety," the patrollers can ask questions related to the content of each video. This reinforces the message and gets the students to voice and remember what they've seen. Such sessions help establish a positive image of the ski patrol. Students will tend to be more receptive to the safety message when they see patrollers on the hill or meeting the bus. They will also better understand why safety is such an important issue.

On the Slopes

Patrollers can improve skier safety on the slopes by marking hazards, by placing skier traffic control signs and fencing, and—more importantly—by actively educating skiers on the mountain. Active education efforts include congratulating or rewarding safe skiers, posting patrollers at special skier education stations on the slopes, and confronting and attempting to reform the reckless skiers. Only about 20 percent of reckless skiers know they are doing something wrong—the other 80 percent simply don't know any better.

Traffic control signs carry various messages, such as "Slow," "Caution," or "Trails Merge." For example, if a run heads abruptly into a lift line or beginner area, a ski patrol member might place a large "Slow" sign a few hundred feet uphill from the merging point. Signs are commercially available with international pictographs, eliminating the need for skiers to read.

A popular type of sign for slow skiing areas is a large piece of plastic fabric supported by plastic poles. The signs can be ordered with any message, but the most commonly used is an orange fabric sign with "Slow" printed in large black letters. Traffic control signs are usually moved off the run at sweep time so grooming equipment can work without dodging the signs or leaving an ungroomed spot.

Some places on a mountain may carry too much traffic or attract advanced skiers, and a mere "Slow" sign might be ineffective. Two popular runs merging

Elementary students are usually receptive to skiing safety messages brought into the school.

near the bottom of a lift, "show-off" spots such as a steep groomed section of run leading into a flatter section, or an advanced run merging into a beginner area – these and other types of places can benefit from effective traffic control.

One way to control skiers at such spots is to place control fencing, or speed traps, across the run so that skiers must turn and slow down to continue down the hill. A speed trap can be built from lengthy plastic fabric banners, or more simply from bamboo poles and red fabric tape or rope. A simple setup consists of three sections, each with enough rope and bamboo to cover more than a third of the run to be controlled. Each section is overlapped in relation to the fall line, with an opening that only allows passage across the fall line. If the speed trap is bamboo with rope, a slow sign placed a hundred feet or so uphill from the maze helps warn skiers of the upcoming obstacle. If large banners form the speed trap, they are quite visible, especially if the banners are printed with "Slow" across

SKI PATROLLER

them. On narrow runs, speed traps must be set up so that skiers aren't heading toward each other as they come out of the maze. Speed traps are usually taken down each night so grooming machines can remove the ruts that inevitably form.

At places where a speed trap would be impractical but some kind of speed control is needed, patrollers may have to stand next to a slow sign during busy times and yell at skiers to slow down. The combination of a slow sign and a patroller verbally reinforcing the message works well – skiers get the impression that the ski area and ski patrol are serious about speed control. The skiers see the sign before they see you, so they at least have some idea that a slow area is coming up.

On a crowded run, though, speed control can be nerve-wracking work. Many skiers will continue to ski too fast past the sign before they realize you are a patroller; others will lose control when they suddenly see that a patroller is watching.

Most skiers are concerned about being mowed down by other skiers, and control fencing is very effective in reducing the number of such incidents. For example, at Winter Park, Colorado, the ski patrol received twenty written complaints from guests about reckless skiers in 1981–82. After implementing a program that combined control fencing with active skier education on the mountain, the patrol received two complaints in 1985–86 and none in 1986–87.

Active skier education on the mountain can take many forms. Some ski areas, such as Winter Park, have sophisticated programs that reward safe skiers with complimentary beverages and require reckless skiers to watch the "Tony's Flight" film or "Ski Sense and Safety" before being allowed to continue skiing. Other patrols may simply confront reckless skiers when they see them.

What you say and your way of saying it when confronting a reckless skier, including body language, are very important. A firm but friendly approach is best. Removing your goggles or sunglasses establishes eye contact with the skier and makes you appear less threatening. If the problem skier is with a group, ask if you can talk with him alone (unless the entire group has been skiing recklessly). A young male skier might feel he has to impress his friends by not taking any guff from the ski patrol. Getting him away from the group lets you talk to him without making him put on a show for his friends. An ideal conversation might go like this:

Patroller: "Excuse me, could I talk to you for a minute?"

Skier: "Yeah, I guess so."

Patroller: "You were skiing too fast up there in the beginner area. We've got it posted with slow skiing signs, and I'd appreciate it if you'd obey the slow signs."

Skier: "I've been skiing this hill for years, and I can handle that run."

Patroller: "That might be true, but there are a lot of skiers on that run who aren't as good as you. One of them could ski in front of you and you'd be going too fast to avoid a collision. We have a policy here of marking the ticket of a fast skier with a red felt tip pen. I need to mark your ticket. It will show other patrollers that you've been warned about skiing fast. If you're caught again, the patroller will take your ticket and you'll be through skiing for the day."

Skier: "That's really dumb. What about all those guys who went down there ahead of me? Are you going to take their tickets too?"

Patroller: "I didn't catch them, I caught you. Maybe if you know those other guys you can tell them that the ski patrol here is on the lookout for fast skiers and that we mark their tickets after we talk to them."

Skier: "So if I get caught going fast again you'll take my lift ticket?"

Patroller: "That's right."

Skier: "Okay, I guess I'll watch out then."

Patroller: "Thanks. See you on the hill."

Of course, this example shows an ideal situation – the skier has been cooperative. Not every reckless skier you confront will be happy about losing ski time to listen to a lecture from the ski patrol. You have to remember that you represent the ski area, and your conduct speaks for your ski area. You become an on-the-hill public relations person, and what you say and do affects not only the reckless skier's impression of the ski area, but that of every other skier who happens to see the confrontation.

Praising safe skiers is obviously a happier experience. You might simply tell the skier that you saw him or her assisting a fallen skier and that your ski area appreciates having courteous skiers as customers. Or, if your area has a program like Winter Park's, you can issue a beverage coupon, button, or other token of the ski area's appreciation. Rewarding or congratulating safe skiers is an ideal opportunity for positive contact between skiers and the ski patrol.

Good Relations with Skiers

Many ski resorts now do all they can to create a quality experience for their guests, and ski patrols have joined with area management to help every skier enjoy a quality skiing experience. In the past, many skiers' only contact with the ski patrol was if they were injured or skiing recklessly, and patrollers tended to be isolated from guests and even from other employees at a ski area. The patrol worked on the mountain, rode the lifts together, and remained a close-knit group.

Ski patrollers, however, are in a unique position to improve public relations for their ski areas. Meeting with skiers continually in a friendly way, knowing the mountain well and the conditions of the day, patrollers, just like ski instructors, are looked at by skiers as "the experts." Every time you ride the ski lift with a skier, you have a chance to talk with the skier and improve the skier's image of both the ski patrol and the ski area. Simply riding the lift and having an ordinary conversation with skiers makes the ski patrol more visible, but you can also steer the conversation in a certain direction and help promote whatever your ski area wants to promote.

In such conversations, simple skiing or safety tips might be all that is considered appropriate. Patrollers usually know where the best skiing of the day can be found, and skiers appreciate getting such tips. In stormy weather, you might suggest runs that are out of the wind or below the fog. Be careful in suggesting runs to skiers, however. Suggesting an expert run to a skier whose ability is unknown to you can lead to a liability problem if the skier is injured on that run. Other tips on stormy days can help the skier see where he's going: keeping goggles clear by using a no-fog cloth, keeping them on your face, and making sure the goggles are in good condition contribute to better vision on foggy days. Skiing on runs with trees gives better depth perception and makes skiing easier. Any tip that will help the skier enjoy his skiing day is worth passing on.

At Snowmass, Colorado, each patroller's workday includes sitting and visiting with skiers in the mountain restaurants. Each patroller spends an hour at a special table reserved for the "Meet the Patrol" program, and skiers are invited to sit and visit with patrollers. At Deer Valley, Utah, patrollers stand outside the summit patrol building to meet skiers and answer questions.

As the ski industry matures and grows more sophisticated in skier education and public relations, so will the ski patrol. Accident prevention and skier education may someday become larger parts of the ski patrol's work than first aid and accident handling. At areas that lead the way in skier education, the benefits of such programs have proven that the cost and effort involved are worthwhile. Reduced accident rates, especially collisions, and reduced complaints from guests concerning reckless skiers show that skier education and reckless-skier control are indeed becoming the ski patrol's most important job.

5

Lift Evacuation

Modern ski lifts are very reliable, but mechanical devices being what they are, lifts still break down from time to time. Often a simple problem is corrected quickly, and the lift is back in operation in minutes. Modern lifts are built with auxiliary power sources to drive them in case of a power failure. Sometimes, though, auxiliary power can't be used. If the haul rope comes off a sheave for some reason (a skier jumping off a chair can do it) or a chair gets entangled with a tower, running the lift on auxiliary can cause further damage or injure passengers on the lift. In such cases the only alternative is to evacuate the lift.

Time is an important factor during any lift breakdown. Skiers on a lift are at the mercy of the weather, and on a cold windy day they can become chilled in less than half an hour of sitting on a disabled lift. Ski area management makes the decision to evacuate a lift by weighing the length of time the lift may be down (disabled) against the effect that amount of time will have on the passengers. Generally, half an hour is the maximum time allowed. If lift personnel and management feel the lift can't be restarted within thirty minutes, an evacuation is initiated. Even when the decision to evacuate is made fairly quickly, an actual evacuation may take an hour or more, so the last skier evacuated can spend well over an hour fighting hypothermia.

Evacuating skiers from a disabled lift puts a big responsibility in your hands. As with a medical emergency, you hold someone's life in your hands – one mistake could cost that person's life. Lift evacuation requires a working knowledge of ropes and knots, specially designed evacuation equipment, and techniques derived from rock climbing.

Self-evacuation is another big responsibility – a risk to your own life. Generally, smaller ski patrols practice and carry the gear for self-evacuation, while larger patrols don't. In the event of a lift breakdown, the small patrol at an area with two or three lifts might have over half its members stranded on a disabled lift, leaving few patrollers to evacuate skiers; the patrol at a large area would have more patrollers spread out on the mountain, leaving more help available for a lift evacuation.

A patrol that practices self-evacuation will usually cache evacuation equipment along the lift line, allowing patrollers who self-evacuate to begin evacuating skiers without waiting for equipment to come down from the summit. Each ski area uses its own combination of the available techniques and equipment, and as with many aspects of ski patrol work, there's no substitute for properly supervised training at the ski area where you will patrol. With the possible exception of knot tying, none of the techniques described in this chapter should be attempted without proper supervision.

Rope Techniques

Rope and knots form the foundation of lift evacuation work, and their importance can't be overemphasized. An improperly tied knot can jam, becoming difficult or impossible to untie. Worse, if an improperly tied knot fails to hold when a load is put on it, that knot endangers you or another skier. I learned this lesson the hard way.

Once in my early days as a patroller, we were practicing self-evacuation. No one had shown me how to tie an overhand bend, so rather than show my

Bight.   Loop.   Half hitch.

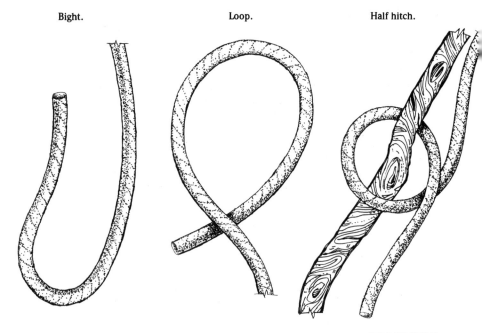

SKI PATROLLER

ignorance I tied the sling with a square knot. The nylon webbing used for tying self-evacuation slings is very slick and won't hold together in a square knot or sheet bend; the overhand bend is a superior knot for tying nylon webbing into a sling.

We got on the lift, rode out until everyone was suspended in the air, then proceeded to self-evacuate. Our self-evacuation kit consists of a seat formed from a loop of nylon webbing and clipped into a carabiner. A light climbing rope is doubled over the lift cable and wrapped through the carabiner. I put my sling on, wrapped my rope through my carabiner, and slid out of the chair. As soon as my full weight was on the sling, it came apart and I flew down the rope hanging on by my gloves. Luckily I wasn't hurt, but I did ruin a pair of ski gloves. I also learned how to tie the overhand bend.

Knots

Strictly speaking, a knot is a configuration in a rope used only to tie that rope to itself. A bend ties two ropes together, and a hitch ties a rope onto another object. Since many bends and hitches are commonly called knots, I may use the word knot to describe a bend or hitch.

A few more terms help describe the ways rope can be bent to form knots:

END. The end, or running end, of a rope is the part of the rope being handled or in which a knot will be tied.

STANDING PART. The standing part is the whole rope except the end mentioned above, and may be unused or fastened elsewhere.

BIGHT. A bight is a bend in a rope in which the rope doesn't cross itself.

LOOP. A loop is a bend in a rope in which the rope crosses itself.

TURN. A turn is a loop that passes around a shaft or another part of the rope.

HALF HITCH. A half hitch is a turn pulled around an object or another part of the rope in such a way as to lock itself.

Two basic knots are often used to form more complex knots, and should be part of your basic knot-tying skills. They are the overhand knot and the figure-eight knot.

Overhand Knot.
The overhand knot is frequently used as a backup to prevent another knot from becoming untied during use. It may also be used to provide a handhold on a rope for climbing or descending, and temporarily to prevent a newly cut rope from unraveling.

Figure-eight Knot.
Unlike the overhand knot, the figure-eight knot is fairly easy to untie when used as a handhold or end stop in a rope. When tied on a bight, the figure-eight forms a strong, easily untied loop for footholds or for tying ropes to evacuation seats.

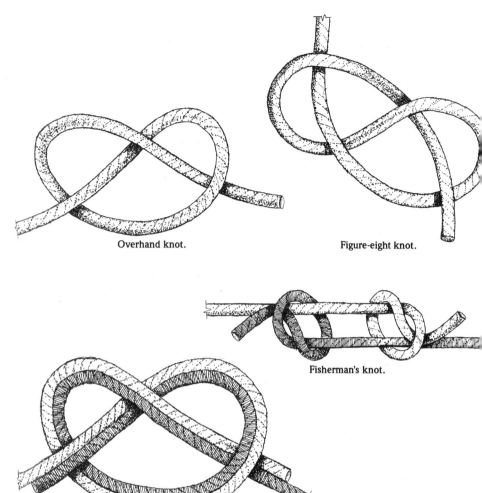

Overhand knot.

Figure-eight knot.

Fisherman's knot.

Overhand bend, or water knot.

More complex knots, such as those described below, serve various purposes in lift evacuation. Some are used more than others, and some ski areas use only one or two of the knots described here.

Overhand Bend.

The overhand bend, also called the water knot, is ideal for tying nylon webbing into slings. The knot is formed by loosely tying an overhand knot in one rope, and then leading the second rope end along the same path in the opposite direction. The overhand bend is easily confused with the fisherman's knot.

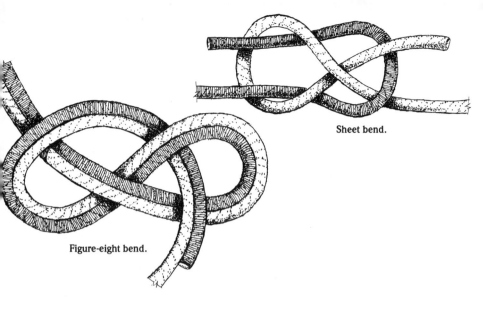

Sheet bend.

Figure-eight bend.

Fisherman's Knot. The fisherman's knot will hold in nylon webbing as long as a load is applied, but the knot can become untied if not secured by extra overhand knots. The fisherman's knot is good for joining two ropes of different sizes or different materials; for instance, for tying a lead line to a rescue rope.

Figure-eight Bend. The figure-eight bend is tied somewhat like the overhand bend, and can be used for similar purposes. It is easier to untie than the overhand bend, but is bulkier and requires more rope. The figure-eight bend is also called the Flemish bend.

Sheet Bend. The sheet bend is good for joining two ropes of different sizes, although it may not hold if the ropes are extremely different in size. Stiff, $7/16$-inch synthetic rescue rope and $1/8$-inch nylon lead line are so different that a sheet bend may not hold them together. A sheet bend can be quickly formed to join two ropes when one already has a loop, such as a bowline, tied in it.

Bowline. The bowline has been called the king of knots. It plays several roles in lift evacuation work, and dozens of additional purposes in climbing, sailing, and any other activity that involves rope and knots. It can be used to attach persons or objects to a line, and when tied on a bight in conjunction with a figure-eight on a bight, forms a rescue seat for evacuating skiers from a lift. Notice in the diagram that the free end of the rope is on the inside of the loop. The knot will hold if tied with the free end outside the loop, but that way it is only half as strong as a properly tied bowline.

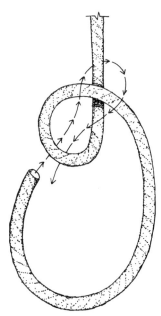

Starting the bowline.

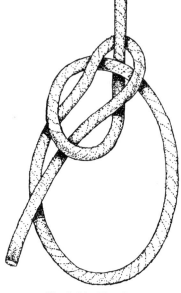

The finished bowline.

Bowline on a Bight.

The bowline on a bight is a rather tricky knot to tie, and for lift evacuation its use is limited to forming an evacuation seat when nothing else is available. To form one that would be useful as a seat, start with a bight about five feet long. Tie the knot as shown in the diagram. The two loops formed should be large enough for ski boots to slip through, and the loops need to slide up the skier's legs to the butt.

Figure-eight on a Bight.

The figure-eight on a bight, or figure-eight loop, is useful for tying rescue ropes to evacuation devices such as tee seats. To tie a rope to the ring on a rescue tee, first loosely tie an ordinary figure-eight with plenty of rope left in the working end. Then pass the working end through the ring and back through the knot along the same path in the opposite direction.

As mentioned, an evacuation can be accomplished with nothing more than a rescue rope. The seat is formed by tying a bowline on a bight that's about five feet long. The two loops formed must be large enough for ski boots to pass through and to slide up to the skier's rear. About a foot above the bowline, tie a figure-eight on a bight large enough to go under one arm and over the opposite shoulder. A bight four feet long is about right – it will take some experimentation to get the right combination of bowline loops and figure-eight loops.

The main disadvantage of the rope rescue seat is that the passenger must remove his skis to get into the seat. For several reasons, it's much better if the skier can be evacuated with his skis on. First, to remove skis while seated in a

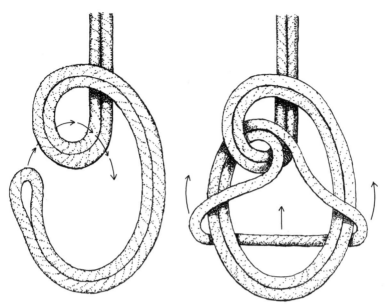

Forming a bowline on a bight.

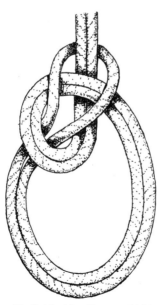

The finished bowline on a bight.

Figure-eight on a bight.

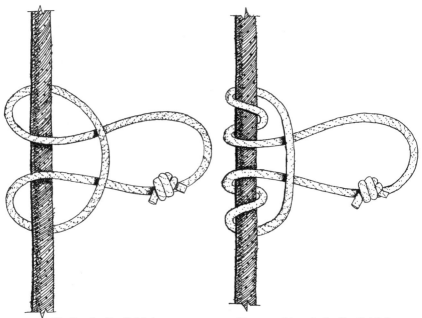

Starting the Prusik hitch.   The second loop in the Prusik hitch.

chair lift, the skier has to lean out over the edge of his seat in a precarious position high above the ground. Second, if the skis aren't lowered on a rope by the rescuers, the skis may land on people below the lift, or else get lost in the snow – moreover, lowering skis takes valuable time and attention.

The finished Prusik hitch.

The Prusik Hitch.

There may be occasions during an evacuation or self-evacuation when you need to climb up the evacuation rope. Perhaps a skier is afraid to get into the evacuation device, or too hypothermic to understand directions. There are several ways to get a patroller up to a chair if plenty of help and extra ropes are available. But if only one rope is available, and little help, a pair of pre-tied loops formed into Prusik hitches can be a lifesaver. Prusik loops can also get you out of a jam if you get stuck halfway down your self-evacuation rope, for example, when your coat gets caught in the rope and carabiner.

In cases like these, a Prusik hitch is wrapped around the evacuation rope. When weight is applied, the Prusik hitch grips a larger rope such as a rescue rope. When the weight is removed, the hitch can be loosened easily and slipped up or down the rope to another position. If you have two short Prusik loops (about one foot long) and a webbing sling, clip your evacuation harness into one Prusik hitch, then slide that Prusik hitch up the rope as far as possible. You rest your feet in the webbing sling, which is about three feet long, that you tie or clip into the other Prusik. To tie the webbing loop into the Prusik, use the ring hitch, which is the basis of the Prusik hitch. If you have an extra carabiner with you, you can use it to clip the webbing sling to the Prusik hitch. If you don't have a webbing sling, you can use two Prusik loops, one about three feet long and another about one foot long. Your feet rest in the long loop and you clip your harness into the short loop.

The loops are made of lengths of 4 or 5mm (1/4" or 5/16") climbing rope. To make a one-foot loop, start with a piece of rope about forty inches long and tie the ends together in an overhand bend. To make a three-foot loop, start with about seven feet of rope and tie the ends in an overhand bend. A long loop made

Climbing a rope using two Prusik hitches and two slings.

of climbing rope costs more than a webbing loop and is heavier—but it is simpler to use. Using two short Prusiks, a webbing sling, and possibly another carabiner means carrying more equipment in your pack. In the end, it's a matter of personal preference, and some patrollers don't even carry Prusik loops.

A wide range of special equipment for lift evacuation is in use across the country. Most lift evacuation equipment and techniques are based on the use of a rope as a means of lowering the stranded skier, although ladders fitted with large

SKI PATROLLER

hooks are effective rescue tools for low spans close to a lift terminal. Much of the rope-related equipment belongs to one of two categories—one category includes all the devices for attaching the skier to the rescue rope; the other category includes all the devices for getting the rescue rope where it's needed.

Evacuation Seats and Slings

Perhaps the most widely used device for attaching skiers to the rescue rope is the evacuation "tee," so called because of its shape. The tee is lightweight, simple, and easy for stranded skiers to use. The simplest device is a sling that just fits under a skier's arms around the chest. It's an inexpensive, lightweight device, but doesn't give the skier much comfort or security. A lightweight, commercially made seat harness is available that gives the skier much better comfort and security than the sling. Still another option is a large canvas or nylon bag. The bag eliminates problems with instructing skiers in its use, and is especially handy

This typical evacuation "tee," held by the skier on the left, is in position for the skier to begin putting his weight on it.

in gondola rescues. Skiers already have their skis off in a gondola, and they can get into the bag in the safety of the gondola car, then be lowered out of the car.

Putting the rescue rope in position can be difficult, and there is a wide variety of equipment available for this purpose. High cable spans and windy weather often make a simple throw of the rope impossible. In relatively good weather on low spans, the rope can be thrown over the cable. Coiling the rope by starting with large coils and working to successively smaller coils, then throwing the entire coil, works surprisingly well.

Light Line

The next most commonly used method involves throwing some form of weight attached to a light line. The light line is called a lead (lēd) line, and the weights attached can be pool balls, baseballs, carabiners, or specially cast metal weights that the line can be wrapped around when not in use. After the lead line has been tossed over the lift cable, the free end of the lead line is tied to the rescue rope and the rescue rope is pulled up and over the lift cable.

Yankee ingenuity has come up with a few devices for getting a lead line over a lift cable that's too high for a simple baseball throw. One, called the Line Slinger, consists of a slingshot with a fishing reel attached. A fishing weight tied to the fishing line is shot over the lift cable. Then the fishing line is tied to a lead line and pulled over the cable. The fishing line can't be attached directly to the rescue rope because the weight of the rescue rope will break the fishing line. Another device was adapted from a dog trainer's dummy-throwing pistol that uses 22-caliber powder charges to shoot a stuffed canvas cylinder. The lead line is simply attached to the canvas cylinder, and both are shot over the lift cable.

When conditions prevent any success with throwing devices, a patroller may be forced to climb the nearest uphill lift tower and place the rescue rope over the lift cable from there. Climbing towers in ski boots is dangerous, and should be done very carefully. A safety harness reduces the danger, but unless tower climbing is standard procedure at a ski area, harnesses may not be available.

When a lift design prevents a simple ground-based rope rescue, it becomes necessary for rescuers to reach stranded passengers more directly. Very high spans present one situation requiring this approach, and gondolas usually require a rescuer in the cabin for an effective evacuation. The new high-speed quad lifts, if fully loaded, will have so many skiers on them at one time that ordinary ground-based rope evacuations will prove too slow. Special cable-riding devices are used for such situations. The devices are commonly called bikes because of the bicycle seats used on some models. The bike typically consists of a framework holding one or two grooved wheels that fit on the lift cable, a fail-safe brake system, and a seat or climbing harness.

A new model designed and built by an Aspen ski patroller includes an attachment point for carabiners, a friction device, rope, and harnesses for lowering skiers, so the rescuer on the bike can effect an evacuation with minimal help from ground crews. Patrollers have become so confident of the new units that they've taken to racing each other down the lift cable in practice sessions.

Rock Climbing Methods

Techniques and equipment borrowed from rock climbing are used not only in actual evacuations, but as backup protection in practice sessions. All of the equipment and methods for self-evacuation can be traced to rock climbing. A rope rescue is basically a belay – a rock climber's safety device – while self-evacuation is derived from rappelling.

Lift evacuation using a "tee" seat. Note how the rope makes three-fourths of a turn around the cable and also rubs against itself.

Once the rescue rope is over the lift cable, and a device for attaching the skier to the rope is on one end of the rope, the rest of the rescue is similar to belaying a descending rock climber from below. First, the weight of the skier on the tee or sling resembles the climber. Second, the rescue rope over the lift cable resembles the climber's rope attachment point above him. Third, the rescuer resembles the belayer, holding tension on the rope to prevent the climber from falling.

As each rescue team of two or three patrollers reaches a chair to be evacuated, each skier (or at least each group in the chair) must be instructed on the procedure that will be used. Ideally, one rescuer can explain the procedure, using the evacuation device to demonstrate, while another rescuer gets in position and prepares to belay the skier. The skier must be instructed not to do anything until told to by the rescuers. Still, it's a good idea for the belayer to be in position and ready to belay well before the evacuation device is pulled up to the chair. An anxious or hypothermic skier might jump or fall onto the evacuation device before being instructed to, and an alert belayer can save an otherwise ugly situation.

The skier's weight on the rope exerts an upward pull on the belayer's end of the rescue rope. The point where the rope passes over the lift cable provides some friction, and that friction can be varied and used to make the belayer's job easier. If the rope simply passes over one side of the cable and down the other, a small amount of friction will be generated, but if the skier being lowered is heavier than the belayer, the belayer can be dragged or even lifted. In that situation, it becomes necessary for a second rescuer to help hold the belayer in place. The second person can simply stand behind the belayer and push down on the sitting belayer's shoulders. Or if the belayer is standing, a webbing sling can be looped around his waist and also around the helper's waist. The helper then sits in the snow behind the belayer.

A good way to increase the friction is to pass the belayer's end of the rope across the downhill side of the skier's end of the rope and then slightly uphill from the point where the rope passes over the lift cable. This creates about three-quarters of a turn around the lift cable. For even more friction, the rope can be wrapped once around itself. A minor disadvantage of wrapping the rope around itself is that after the evacuation of each chair someone needs to unwind the wraps so the rope can be moved along the cable to the next chair.

The point where the rope passes over the cable can be a problem on some types of lifts. The chair grip (the attachment of the chair to the lift cable), if it is an external type, may have a narrow point of metal extending uphill from the main part of the grip, and there may be a slight gap between that part of the grip and the cable. The part of the grip is sometimes called a duckbill because of its shape. Rescuers need to be aware that the rescue rope can lodge between the duckbill and the cable, jamming the rescue rope and possibly damaging it. Some ski areas use a device called the Line Saver to prevent the rope from being jammed under the grip. The Line Saver also protects the rope from the wear caused by passing over the lift cable repeatedly. The disadvantage of the Line Saver is that it reduces friction at the point where the rope passes over the cable, although the rope can still be wrapped around itself to gain friction.

Wayne Ellington, Pro Patrol Director at Showdown Ski Area in Montana, invented a way to gain friction using Line Savers without wrapping the rope around itself. Wayne welded a piece of metal rod about sixteen inches long to each of his Line Savers. The rods have an eye formed in the ends that the rope passes through. Then the rope is wrapped around the rod two or three times, through the Line Saver, and down to the evacuation device.

One difference between the climber's belay and a belay for lift evacuation is that the climber's belay is intended to stop a fall, while the lift evacuation belay provides a controlled descent for the skier. There are two methods of controlling the skier's descent. One, the body belay, simply uses the belayer's hands and body in such a way that some friction is gained and the descent controlled. The other, the mechanical belay, uses a climber's descending (rappelling) device. Most patrols that belay with a descending device use a figure-eight descender. The descender is clipped into a carabiner that is also clipped into some type of climbing harness.

In the body belay, the rope runs from the lift cable to the belayer's right hand, across the belayer's back, and into the left hand. Your right hand only rests on the rope as you keep your right arm slightly bent to prevent the rope from sliding up and over your shoulders. Your left hand controls the skier's descent. By extending your left arm and letting the rope run through your hands, you can lower the skier fairly easily.

The figure-eight descender provides enough friction for you to control the skier's descent by varying your grip on the rope with one hand. The mechanical belay with a descender requires less effort than the body belay, but does involve more equipment. If the rescue rope doesn't provide enough friction, requiring the belayer to be anchored, then the harness used for attaching the descender can also be used for anchoring the belayer. The helper simply sits behind the belayer and holds onto the harness or sling.

For a safety belay during practice sessions, the practice "victim" ties the safety rope snugly in a bowline around his waist. An experienced belayer should always be on the safety belay when others practice lift evacuation or self-evacuation.

Self-Evacuation

Self-evacuation more closely resembles the climbing technique from which it was borrowed than does any other lift evacuation technique. Rappelling is a way for a climber, using a rope, to quickly descend a section of rock that may have taken hours to climb. Self-evacuation is a way for a patroller, using a rope, to quickly abandon a stalled lift and begin evacuating skiers.

The diaper sling is a device used by climbers to attach themselves to the rope. It is sometimes used with a waist sling or chest harness. For lift evacuation, the diaper sling is used alone. To provide friction, climbers use a complex combination of carabiners, a figure-eight descender, or a carabiner brake bar. For lift evacuation, most patrollers either use a figure-eight descender or simply wrap the evacuation rope around a carabiner three or four times.

Proper position for a sitting body belay.

Some ski patrols no longer practice self-evacuation because of the risk involved, and the practice is not recognized or recommended by the National Ski Patrol. It is included here because some patrols do still practice self-evacuation. Again, the purpose of this book is entertainment and education, and it cannot replace proper instruction from qualified instructors. Self-evacuation must be practiced only with proper supervision and training.

The first step in self-evacuation is to toss your rope over the lift cable. Your rope should be at least twice as long as the highest span of any lift you might have to abandon. Find the center of the rope and put it on the lift cable so both halves of the rope are the same length. Take care to avoid getting your rope jammed under the duckbill. It saves time to find the center of the rope ahead of time and mark it with a piece of tape. Be sure the rope hangs free and isn't tangled or knotted. You don't want to rappel into midair and find a knot halfway down your rope.

Forming the three loops to make a diaper sling.

Because patrollers must fit their self-evacuation ropes into a first aid pack or vest, the ropes generally have a smaller diameter than a rock climber would consider safe for rappelling. It has been recommended that a 6mm rope be discarded after one evacuation, but even a 5mm climbing rope, which is considered safe for lift evacuation, has a breaking strength of over 1000 pounds. This is a matter where local custom dictates what equipment you use and how you use it.

To form a diaper sling, you need a length of one-inch-wide nylon webbing from ten to fifteen feet long. Tie the webbing into a loop using an overhand bend. It's best to tie the knot and leave the webbing in loop form while carrying it, leaving one less thing to do when you need the sling. To form the diaper sling:

1. Pass the loop behind you.
2. Hold the two ends in one hand.
3. With the other hand, reach behind you and pull one side of the loop down under your rear end to your crotch.
4. Reach between your legs and pull the webbing up so it reaches the other ends you hold.
5. You should now have three loops in your hand, and one part of the webbing should be around the small of your back with the other around both upper legs and through your crotch.
6. Clip all three loops into a locking carabiner.

A more secure diaper sling can be formed by starting with a longer loop than for the ordinary diaper sling. After reaching between your legs and pulling that loop up, thread it first through one of the side loops, then the other. The remaining length of the center loop must be long enough to tie an overhand knot around the ends of the side loops and through its own center. Clip the single loop into a locking carabiner.

LIFT EVACUATION

Your personal preference or local custom will determine whether you use one or two locking carabiners. Local custom may also require a figure-eight descender. If two carabiners are used, one is simply clipped into the other. Then the rope is wrapped through the upper carabiner. The gates of both carabiners should be up; that is, when the carabiner is opened, the opening should be on top and the hinge should be on the bottom. To wrap the rope through the carabiner, hold the carabiner and open the gate with one hand. With the other hand, take the doubled rope (remember, it's doubled over the lift cable) at about the level of your chin. Holding the carabiner as high as the sling permits, wrap the rope through the carabiner three times so you get two full wraps of the rope around the straight part of the carabiner. When you're certain that the wraps are right, lock the carabiner gate.

Next, take any slack out of the system by sliding the carabiner up the rope until the sling is taut and there's no slack in the rope above. Then take the free end of the rope and put it to the left of your legs. Take hold of the rope with your left hand. Then reach under your thighs with your right hand and grab the standing part of the rope. Pull the rope under your thighs. Then scoot it back until it's behind your back. You should now have a hold on the rope similar to that in a belay: the rope should pass from your carabiner under your left arm and across your back, then under your right arm to your right hand. Your right hand is your braking hand, and your left hand keeps you away from the chair seat when you first go below it, then keeps the carabiner away from your clothing. You hold the sling to do this, instead of holding the carabiner or the rope.

If you use a figure-eight descender, it's not necessary to wrap the rope behind you. It can pass directly from the descender, which is clipped into a locking carabiner along with your sling, to your braking hand. The reason for passing the rope behind your back when using a carabiner is to gain friction, and the figure-eight descender provides enough friction of its own. To attach the figure-eight descender to the rope, you have to remove the descender from the carabiner. Form a bight in the rope. Pass it through the large hole in the descender, then over the smaller ring.

After attaching the rope to your carabiner or descender and getting the proper handhold on your rope, double-check everything in the system. Check your rope to make sure the center is over the cable, or within a few inches of it. Make sure your rope hasn't slipped under the duckbill, and check below you for tangles. Be sure your sling is made correctly and properly clipped into the carabiner. Be sure your carabiner is locked, and be sure your rope is properly attached to the carabiner or descender. Any long hair, scarves, or other loose clothing must be inside a hat or coat, and your coat should be zipped. Getting long hair or loose clothing caught in your rope and carabiner will stop you in midair, and may cause injury. Also put your gloves back on before descending, as the rope can burn your hands.

After you have double-checked every part of your equipment, you are ready to lower yourself. Start by holding the rope in your brake hand, and slowly ease out over the edge of the seat while holding the rope tight. Use your other hand to hold yourself away from the chair. Once all the slack is out of the rope and sling, slowly lower yourself. After you're below the chair, use your non-braking hand to hold your sling away from your chest. Don't hold onto the braking carabiner or figure-eight descender—you could get a finger or a glove caught and become stranded. It's a good idea to carry a pair of Prusik loops for such an emergency. The Prusik can be used to take your weight off the braking device and allow you to free the tangle. A smooth descent is best, and you should avoid stopping. As soon as you reach the ground, get your rope free of your braking device and pull your rope down from the cable.

Evacuation Plans

An efficient lift evacuation is no accident—it's the result of careful planning and teamwork by patrollers, lift personnel, and ski area management. A typical lift evacuation plan spells out who decides to evacuate the lift, who is in charge, and how patrollers and lift personnel are to be notified of an evacuation. It also spells

A patroller self-evacuates from the lift using a carabiner and diaper sling.

out who will participate in the evacuation, what techniques and equipment will be used, and where the equipment is stored. A good plan outlines the proper sequence of events, beginning with a lift failure, on through every stage of the evacuation to a post-evacuation critique. A critique helps management refine the plan by showing weak spots in the operation or plan.

Another function of the plan is to give patrollers a way to stay familiar with their ski area's methods and equipment. Part of each practice session includes reviewing the plan and checking equipment. Although every ski area's plan and procedures vary according to the area's needs, the general sequence of events for a chair lift evacuation is as follows:

1. The lift is declared inoperable, and management decides to order an evacuation.
2. One patroller skis along the lift line and informs the passengers that the lift can't be started and an evacuation is in progress. If the patrollers on the lift are trained and equipped for self-evacuation, they begin to do so.
3. All available trained help gathers at a predetermined place (usually wherever lift evacuation equipment is cached) to receive instructions and begin the evacuation. Each team is assigned a portion of the lift line to evacuate, then gathers its equipment, inspects it, and begins evacuating skiers.
4. Rescue teams start by getting the rescue rope over the lift cable, then arranging the rope so there will be enough friction and the belayer will have a tangle-free rope to let out when he lowers the skier.
5. One rescuer demonstrates and explains to the stranded skiers how to use the evacuation device.
6. The skiers are told to throw down their poles. Then the evacuation device is pulled up to the chair.
7. The skier gets on or in the evacuation device while the belayer stays alert and keeps tension on the rope.
8. When the skier is in the evacuation device, he slides out of the chair, and the belayer lowers the skier to the ground. When the skier reaches the ground, one rescuer turns the skier so his skis are across the fall line. The skier is helped out of the evacuation device, and his name is recorded.
9. When one chair is evacuated, the rope is moved past that chair to the next one. The rescuers may need to use a whipping motion with a rescuer on either side of the lift cable to move the rope past a chair. In extreme cases, it may be necessary to use a "line flipper"—a carabiner taped to a bamboo pole—or to pull the rope down and rethrow it in front of the next chair. The team continues until all chairs have been evacuated.
10. A patroller skis the lift line to make sure that all skiers have been evacuated from the chair and that no lift evacuation or self-evacuation equipment is left dangling from the cable.

If you're a rock climber, you should have no trouble with lift evacuation. If you are afraid of heights, you might not enjoy self-evacuation or climbing lift towers to place rescue ropes. If you're like most patrollers, though, you'll become comfortable working at heights, and even learn to enjoy the adrenaline rush that comes with rescues and practice sessions that leave you dangling from a rope.

6

Search and Rescue

At 2:00 p.m. one stormy February day, Allen Smith's father reported to the Grand Targhee ski patrol that Allen was lost. Twelve-year-old Allen wasn't wearing a hat, and the weather was at its worst—snowing an inch an hour with winds twenty-five to thirty miles per hour. Allen's father said they had been skiing together at the top of Arrowhead when they split up, planning to meet at the bottom. Allen never showed up.

Ski patrols often get reports of missing skiers at 2:00 or 3:00 in the afternoon. Usually the lost person is simply skiing on another lift or is at the base area. It's impossible to follow up on every misplaced person reported during regular hours, but his father was certain that Allen was lost. One patroller began searching on the mountain, while another searched along the ski area boundary and Allen's father was sent to thoroughly search the base area—cafeteria, video game room, rest room, parking lot. This process is called the "bastard search." It's the patrol's first response to a lost-skier report.

At 4:30, with sweep completed, Allen still hadn't been found. We began an intensive search of the ski area boundaries near where Allen had last been seen. Usually ski tracks are easy to spot in Grand Targhee's soft snow, but it had been snowing hard all day. We called in the county sheriff and again searched the ski area around where Allen had last been seen. Given Allen's age, his experience (this was his first time at Grand Targhee), and the heavy snow, this was a high urgency situation that called for the quickest response possible.

Sheriff's Deputy Tracy Hansen arrived at about 5:45 with Blitz, his German shepherd search dog. Four inches of snow had fallen between 1:00 and 4:00 p.m., the wind was still blowing hard, and we still had found no tracks leading out of the ski area. Even though we couldn't find his tracks, we had to consider the possibility that Allen was going downhill, away from the ski area. We also had to make sure he wasn't still on the mountain, injured, or hiding under a tree. We desperately needed a clue that would tell us where Allen had gone.

As part of a basic search tactic—defining or limiting the search area—Deputy Hansen sent searchers on snowmobiles up the canyon below the part of the ski area where Allen had last been seen. If Allen had kept going downhill, they would likely cross his tracks. If they didn't cross his tracks, we would know that he hadn't reached the bottom of the canyon – at least not yet.

At 6:15 we still had found no clues as to where Allen had gone. It was nearly dark, and the wind was still howling. We took Allen's father up the mountain on skis, and he pointed out the exact spot where he had last seen Allen. Blitz the search dog was brought to the spot and given a tennis shoe of Allen's to sniff. The dog could find no scent of Allen in the strong wind. Finally, at 6:45, the snowmobile searchers in the canyon found Allen curled up under a tree. He had abandoned his skis, waded through a creek several times, and on our arrival was in the second stage of hypothermia. The searchers put dry clothes on him and took him to a waiting ambulance. A doctor examined him soon afterwards and released him the same night.

When a Report Comes In

Any lost-person report demands an immediate response. If you are the first patroller to hear about a lost person, you need to know what to say and what questions to ask. If your ski area uses a questionnaire for gathering information about the lost person, the first report is the time to start filling out that form. The lost person's clothing and equipment, age, experience, and related details help determine how urgent the initial search will be. Getting the lost person's name allows people who don't know him or her to help in the bastard search, and searchers will need to shout the lost person's name when searching outdoors.

The bastard search is an important element in any lost-persons search. The precise origin of the name "bastard search" is uncertain, but it could come from the name searchers want to call the lost person when he is found somewhere comfortable – at home or in a restaurant, for example – when he has been presumed lost. The purpose of the bastard search is to make certain there really is a lost person.

After getting the information needed for a bastard search (name, age, height, weight, clothing, experience), notify whoever will be in charge of the search. Impress on the person reporting to you how important it is for that reporter to stay in contact with you. If possible, keep the individual with you. You must know if the lost person shows up during the bastard search, and if the person reporting to you should leave after finding the "lost" person, you might have no way of knowing what happened to either of them. You also want to prevent the person reporting to you from going out searching and getting lost.

Search Manager

Someone, such as the ski patrol director, area manager, or county sheriff, must be in charge of any search operation. An unmanaged search usually ends in chaos. The search manager should stay at the search headquarters. His main tools are maps of the area, a standardized search plan, radios, and telephones. He decides on search strategy and tactics, appoints people to handle various jobs, and decides where various resources (dogs, snowmobiles, skiers) will be used.

The search manager's first action after the bastard search is organized should be to determine the urgency of the search. If the bastard search has been unsuccessful and the search manager decides the search has a high urgency, he must do several things fairly fast. First he must decide what resources will be needed and establish the probable boundaries of the search area. At most ski areas, the resources immediately available are patrollers on Alpine and cross-country skis, snowmobiles with skilled operators, and perhaps search dogs and their handlers.

Boundaries of the Search

While patrollers get ready to go, the search manager establishes the probable boundaries of the search area. He considers the terrain, the time since the person was lost, the distance the person may have traveled, the history of other searches in the area, and any clues that may have already been found. He also follows his intuition and tries to imagine himself in the lost person's shoes.

The "probable search area" starts as a circle drawn on a map. The size of the circle is determined by the time the lost person has been missing and the person's type of transportation (in our case, on skis). The search manager, knowing that lost skiers rarely climb uphill when first lost, eliminates from the probable search area all places higher up than the last seen point. Once the probable search area has been established, the next step is to attempt to prevent the subject from traveling outside that area, and to find clues (ski tracks) that will help the search manager deduce where the subject has gone.

Alpine skiers, when lost, tend to do what's easiest – go downhill. They will do so for miles, through deep dark woods and thick underbrush, rather than hike back uphill to the ski area. They also do things common to many lost persons. They become irrational, sometimes discarding equipment or clothing. Hypothermia compounds their unclear thinking and irrational behavior. A lost person will expend a large amount of energy, especially on skis, and will usually keep moving until hypothermia or darkness sets in.

Search Methods

As a patroller and potential member of a clue-conscious "hasty team," you should know the value of a good clue. Finding a lone ski track leading out of your ski area boundary is a relatively good clue, and tells you and the search manager not only where the lost person might be but where he probably isn't. Knowing where the lost person is not eliminates large portions of the probable search area and allows more intensive efforts in more likely areas. You can't always be sure a track leading out of the ski area is the lost person's track, however.

There may be other people's tracks around the same area, and in fact the lost person may have strayed off by following the tracks of other skiers who knew their way back to the ski area. If you can find a hat, candy wrapper, or other item that the lost person was known to have, a questionable clue like a ski track among other tracks becomes much more valuable. If a searcher does find a candy wrapper or other seemingly insignificant clue, the information gathered on the lost-persons questionnaire gains importance. Each item on the questionnaire is considered a clue as is any evidence found in the field.

After establishing the probable search area, the search manager sends teams of searchers to look for tracks and other clues. A patroller on skis will look for tracks leading out of the ski area, while snowmobile operators are sent farther out to look for tracks leading out of the (larger) probable search area. Assuming no tracks are found leading out of the probable search area at likely places such as creek drainages, the snowmobile searchers may be instructed to stay at those likely places as perimeter guards. A perimeter guard makes sure the lost person doesn't leave the probable search area undetected and tries to attract the lost person by making noise or creating a source of light such as a fire.

Meanwhile, those searching for tracks leading out of the ski area need to be aware of the freshness of any tracks they find. If the skier has been missing only two or three hours, the track will appear fresh unless heavy snow has fallen. Experienced hasty searchers can judge the age of a track in a snowstorm by the amount of snow in the track.

Certain places are particularly likely to furnish clues; these include creek drainages, canyons, and ridgetops. Roads or cabins might also have attracted the lost person, or hazardous cliffs might have caused that person to become injured and therefore immobile.

Following the lost person's suspected route is an accepted search tactic. If you have several sets of tracks going down a likely creek drainage, but only one lost person, you really have no choice but to follow those tracks until you find more clues or the lost person. Similarly, if you suspect a track that is partly filled in by drifting snow, you may need to use the technique called sign cutting or track cutting. In sign cutting, one member of the hasty team stays where the track disappears while the other member or members cut ahead in expanding semicircles looking for a continuance of the track. No matter which direction the subject has gone, they are likely to pick up the track somewhere. Once a team member finds the track again, he stays with the track while the other team members leapfrog him, circling ahead and continuing to look for the track.

Clothing and Equipment

Proper clothing and equipment are essential if you want to be an effective searcher and avoid the same hazards faced by the lost person, and a searcher should be prepared to spend the night either searching or guarding a search perimeter. In a winter environment, this implies an equipment list of:

- Proper layered clothing including hat, dry gloves, and goggles (goggles should have clear lenses, if possible, for night searches)
- Headlamp with extra batteries

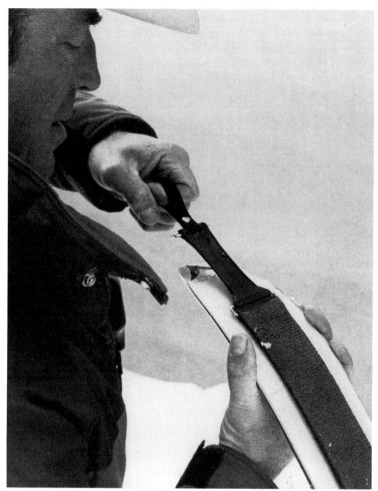

Attaching climbing skins to Alpine skis.

- Two-way radio
- Rucksack with extra clothing and, if available, sleeping bag (for warming a hypothermic lost person)
- Candy, nuts, or other high energy food items, and water or other liquids
- Matches
- Avalanche beacon (if appropriate)
- Compass
- Maps of the search area (these should be provided by the search manager, and may have your assigned search area outlined)
- Climbing skins for the skis

SEARCH AND RESCUE   89

Climbing skins are useful whether you search on Alpine or Nordic skis. Before the days of synthetic materials, climbing skins were made from sealskin. Modern climbing skins are strips of synthetic "hair" on adhesive-backed strips, with clips at each end to help hold the skins on your skis. The hair lies flat so your ski will slide forward, then grips the snow when you weight the ski. If the lost person is able to walk, an extra pair of climbing skins can come in very handy if the person, after being found, needs to hike back. If no extras are available, two searchers can each give one skin to the lost person and the party can limp back to civilization.

When the Person Is Found

Once you find the lost person, you should notify the search manager immediately, and then assess the found person's condition. If he is injured or hypothermic, administer the appropriate first aid. After you attend to the patient's injuries and know your exact location, you can report to the search manager in detail so he can make plans for evacuating the patient. If the person is able to ski, evacuation may simply be a matter of picking a safe route and skiing to the nearest road or snowmobile. If the person is injured or hypothermic, or if evacuating him might endanger the rescuers, then the search manager will need to consider other factors, such as the safety of the person and rescuers, the available equipment and people, the terrain, and the weather.

Searching for lost skiers isn't glamorous. It is often exhausting and dangerous. A successful search rewards you only with the knowledge that you've helped save a life. Even if you didn't personally find the lost person, you've done your part. When you're involved in a search, you're working for the lost person. So if you like mysteries, you'll love winter searches.

Search Dogs and Their Handlers

A trained search dog can be a great asset to any ski patrol. With their excellent sense of smell, dogs can quickly find things a human searcher would take hours to find, or never find at all. A person searching in the dark could easily overlook a cigarette butt, candy wrapper, or other item left by a lost person; a search dog can find such an item by scent.

Everyone leaves behind a trail of microscopic "scent particles" – tiny pieces of skin, hair, and molecules of body odor. A dog's nasal passages contain recesses that permit accumulation of these scent particles that even a dog may not recognize in a single sniff. When on lost-persons searches, an experienced search dog handler uses his or her knowledge of air currents, of the weather, and of the dog to know where to continue the search. On avalanche searches, air currents and weather play a smaller part, and the handler's ability to "read" the dog becomes critical. The scent of a person buried in an avalanche rises slowly through the snow, carried by the person's body heat. The scent comes to the surface directly above the buried person, and an avalanche dog making a "find" will eagerly dig in the snow once he finds the strongest scent.

When a track disappears in drifting snow a trained search dog can often find it with little difficulty. If the track isn't too old and if the wind isn't too strong and isn't blowing in the wrong direction, a search dog will instantly be able to follow the scent left behind by the lost person. If some item belonging to the lost person is available, so much the better.

Today's search dogs are trained to follow the scent of a lost person. The two basic ways a dog searches are *tracking* and *air scenting.* In tracking, the dog follows scents left on the ground or snow. In air scenting, the dog sniffs the air, following the scent in a direct line toward the source. Scent moves downwind from its source in an expanding, but weakening, cone shape. The dog will range back and forth, sniffing the air and changing directions when the scent disappears. The dog handler stays behind the dog, encouraging him and interpreting the dog's actions. A good dog handler knows when the dog is on a scent trail, whether the scent is on the ground or in the air. By definition, experienced dog handlers are experienced searchers, and they come prepared to spend several days outdoors whatever the season.

Ski patrol experience provides you with an excellent background for becoming a search dog handler, and many search dog handlers become involved with search dog work as an extension of their ski patrol skills and interests. For example, Rocky Mountain Rescue Dogs, Inc. (RDI), a nonprofit volunteer organization, was started when two ski patrollers became interested in training their dogs for avalanche rescue. Dick Epley of Ogden, Utah, and John Pickup of Orem, Utah, founded RDI in 1980 when they realized that just one or two handlers and their dogs couldn't respond to the growing number of search operations in their area. An organization was needed to coordinate dog handlers with agencies needing search dogs, and to arrange transportation.

RDI sets training standards for its members and prospective members, and tests teams. The tremendous amount of time, effort, and expertise that go into training a dog make the process almost impossible without the help of a group like RDI. Groups similar to RDI throughout the country help members and prospective members with training. Like ski patrols, search dog groups hold monthly sessions to help members hone their skills, and retesting and certification continue from month to month. Also like ski patrols, search dog groups become more than a way for members to train for their volunteer work. Weekend training sessions become social events as well as workouts, and most of the groups publish monthly newsletters.

Of course, a prospective dog handler must love dogs, but training a search dog also requires the time to work with your dog daily. One or two hours during the week after work, with much longer sessions on weekends, are necessary for you to achieve the level of training and rapport with your dog needed for search work. One active RDI member estimates that almost one-quarter of the people who undertake the project of training search dogs give up the first year.

Medium-sized working breeds make the best search dogs. A small dog can't cover long distances easily, while very large dogs don't fit easily into helicopters,

A Jackson Hole patroller in a practice session with his avalanche dog. *Wade McKoy photo.*

small planes, and other forms of transportation used in search work. German shepherds, golden retrievers, and Labrador retrievers are the most popular breeds for search work. Some dedicated trainers have done well with bloodhounds. Undeniably, bloodhounds have excellent noses, but they are difficult to work "off-lead" – the preferred method for lost-person and avalanche search work.

Choosing a puppy that will be right for you and will become a good search dog is very important. The best puppy for search work is "bright." The pup should be eager and intelligent, with no fear of people. The ideal pup for you may attract you in ways you can't describe, but all other things being equal, that attraction may be the deciding factor.

The best time to begin training a puppy is when the pup is seven to nine weeks old. Dogs up to a year old can be started on search training successfully, but by starting with a young pup you gain an enormous advantage over training an older dog. If you start when the pup is young, you are an important part of his first impressions of the world. You can mold the pup into a dog that will know you and your moods instinctively and will have lifelong training with a search perspective.

The pup's early training consists mostly of socialization, basic obedience, and simple problem solving. Socialization is the process of getting the pup used to being around people and other dogs. A search dog must go up to strangers with no fear – a dog who becomes afraid of strangers is useless as a search dog. A search dog often travels and works with other search dogs, and should be familiar with other dogs so that every new dog isn't a novelty he must investigate.

Your pup should begin to learn words from you at an early age. An easy way to start with a young pup is to watch the pup when you spend time with him around the house. When you see the pup about to sit down, for example, say the word "Sit" in a firm voice. If the pup is about to lie down, say "Down." This way even if you don't formally start obedience training for several weeks, your dog is used to different words and has some idea of their meaning.

You can begin problem solving by simply teaching the pup to get his toys from his toy box himself. Other problems you can encourage a young pup to solve himself are pushing open a door that's slightly ajar, getting in and out of cardboard boxes with the sides cut down, and running through mazes made of furniture.

Some ski patrols will support your efforts in training a search dog. If you show the dedication and hard work necessary to pass certification tests of recognized search dog groups, you have made a worthwhile accomplishment that deserves recognition.

The book *Search Dog Training,* by Sandy Bryson, contains all the information you need to select and begin training a search dog. To find the search dog unit nearest you, contact National Association for Search and Rescue, SAR Dog Committee, P.O. Box 39, Somerset, CA 95484.

7

Avalanche Forecasting, Hazard Reduction, and Rescue

A storm moving into the mountains means different things to different people. For the snowplow driver or truck driver, it means hazardous driving conditions and slower travel. For the farmer, it means being closer to having the irrigation water he needs the following summer. Even among skiers, the approach of a storm provokes different emotions. The powder skier looks forward to stormy weather, while the intermediate skier prefers sunny skies and groomed runs. The area manager would rather see the storm wait until midweek, because stormy weather keeps weekend skiers home. Ski patrollers are torn between their love of powder skiing and the knowledge that a storm means work. At many western ski areas a storm means avalanche work.

Every winter, avalanches around the world kill people and damage property. Even where they don't come into contact with human activity, avalanches are a major force in shaping mountain ranges. A large avalanche takes trees, rocks, and anything else in its path and deposits them at its bottom, or run-out zone.

Sixty-seven percent of recreation-related avalanche accidents in the United States occur outside ski area boundaries. Many lift skiers who are killed in avalanches were outside those boundaries when they were caught. Avalanche accidents in developed ski areas are relatively rare; the credit is due largely to the efforts of ski patrols and other avalanche workers.

How to Analyze Conditions and Reduce Avalanche Probability

To ensure the skiing public's safety, the ski patrol must decide which slopes might avalanche, then release potential avalanches before skiers are on the slopes. Keeping skiers out of avalanche areas until hazard reduction measures are complete often involves closing those areas, then opening them when conditions permit. Avalanche hazard reduction work can be exciting, even awe-inspiring at times. Other times it's just cold, wet, tiring, and dangerous work.

The wind, blowing from right to left in the photo, picks up snow off this peak and deposits it below the left-hand ridge.

The amount of new snow and wind action required to create avalanche conditions depends on the individual ski area – the steepness of its slopes, its weather history for the season, and conditions within the snowpack. The forecaster's tools include experience, an observant eye, good weather information, and data from snowpits dug by workers on the slope. Ski patrollers aren't expected to forecast the weather, but a basic grasp of some weather principles will help you understand how and where avalanche conditions may develop.

Most natural avalanches occur during a storm or soon afterwards, since storms are always depositing new snow on the slopes, or "loading" them. When a moderately strong wind blows over mountain ridges, it accelerates as it blows up the slope, then decelerates as it blows downslope. As the wind accelerates upslope, it picks up snow particles from the surface. Snow is deposited where the wind decelerates over lee slopes, so it's typical for a major avalanche path to be in the lee of prevailing storm winds. A gully or bowl in the lee of storm winds can accumulate snow at a very rapid rate. In a test at Berthoud Pass in Colorado, snow was deposited in a lee gully at the rate of 45 cm (18 inches) per hour.*

Where the wind transports snow across a ridgetop, snow deposits in layers that overhang each other and gradually build into a cornice. At the same time, gravity works to pull the formation downward. A fully formed cornice graphically illustrates the plastic properties of snow. Snow will bend, stretch, or compress if

---

* Perla, Ronald and M. Martinelli, *Avalanche Handbook* (Fort Collins, Col.: USDA Forest Service, 1976), 27.

force is applied slowly. If force is applied quickly, however, by heavy new snowfall or the weight of a skier, the result can be an avalanche.

Snowfall can be measured and recorded in several ways. Avalanche workers daily record total depth of the snowpack, 24-hour new snow and its water equivalent, and the total of new snow and water equivalent for each storm.

Records are also kept for wind speed and direction, temperature (minimum and maximum for the previous 24 hours), and barometric pressure. Wind sensors are usually located on a ridgetop where they will record typical mountain winds. The sensors can be connected to pen-and-graph recorders or computers.

The moment a snowflake lands, it begins to change shape and attach itself to its neighbors. Weather conditions throughout the winter and the depth of the snowpack help determine whether the snow particles in any one layer of the snowpack will become more or less attached to their neighbors (become cohesive or cohesionless). By digging snowpits, avalanche workers attempt to recognize the varying levels of cohesion and snow density that exist in layers in the snowpack, and the relationships between those layers.

The relationship of the layers in a snowpack determines whether or not an avalanche is probable. For example, consider a two-foot-thick soft slab (a slab is any relatively thick, cohesive layer in the snowpack, especially one deposited by the wind) resting on top of a thin layer of loose, cohesionless snow that, in turn, rests on a hard slab. The top slab may need only a small trigger – the weight of a skier or a few inches of new snow may cause it to slide. As with any other field of endeavor, you see the subtle things only after becoming familiar with the obvious. Spending time on skis week after week, with an eye toward varying condi-

Cornice buildup on the lee side of a ridge.

Checking water equivalent of new snow on the weighing rain gauge.

tions, gives you a feel for different types of snow and the weather patterns associated with those types of snow.

A winter's experience at a ski area will give you a chance to see which conditions lead to avalanches at that area. Several storms, each dropping eight inches of snow at 26 degrees Fahrenheit with ten-mile-per-hour winds, may still create varying levels of avalanche potential. Ten miles per hour of wind from one direction may create moderate to high avalanche hazard, while ten miles per hour from the opposite direction creates no avalanche hazard. Also, the length of time the wind blows affects conditions. Winds that blow ten miles per hour all night create more avalanche hazard than winds that stop or change direction halfway through the storm.

Staying alert to clues can give you an excellent feel for avalanche conditions. Recent avalanches on nearby slopes tell you that the avalanche potential on

SKI PATROLLER

Typical wind speed and direction sensors mounted on a tower. Heat lamps help prevent ice buildup.

similar slopes is high. Evidence of wind loading, such as smooth "pillows," cornices on the lee side of ridges, and drift patterns on the snow surface and around trees, indicates the possibility of increased stress on the snowpack on lee slopes. If the snow makes a hollow, drumlike sound as you ski over it, that may indicate unstable conditions. Such sounds are typically a sign of a hard wind slab that has formed over cohesionless snow. Another sound you should be alert for is a sort of "whumph" sound that snow makes when it settles rapidly or when a weak layer within the snowpack collapses.*

"Whumphing" sounds are signs of extreme instability. You should stay away from even mildly steep slopes when you hear settling noises in the snow. Similarly, cracks forming in the snow as you traverse a slope provide direct evidence of instability. If the slope is steep and the cracks deep, you probably shouldn't be there.

Snowpit Tests

Digging a "hasty pit" is a quick way to confirm or deny any suspicions you have concerning the snowpack. To dig one, you'll need a lightweight shovel and a plastic card such as a credit card. Also, a small paintbrush and magnifying glass

---

* Fesler, Doug and Jill Fredston, "Stability Evaluation," in *National Avalanche School Textbook* (Reno, Nev.: National Avalanche School, 1985), 6.2.2, 6.2.4.

are handy, as are the commercially available snowpit cards printed with helpful reminders for snowpit work.

Ideally, your pit should be at a spot that has the same steepness, elevation, and aspect (faces the same direction) as the slope in question. Don't dig your pit where you could start an avalanche, burying yourself or others. Most avalanches start on slopes with a steepness between thirty and forty-five degrees. This doesn't mean that slopes with more than forty-five degrees or less than thirty degrees of slant are necessarily safe. Extremely wet avalanches have killed people on slopes as shallow as ten degrees, while large amounts of snow can cling to very steep slopes until something triggers an avalanche. Use caution, and don't ski alone in suspected avalanche areas. Ridgetops are the safest routes in avalanche areas; avoid gullies and bowls, as you are vulnerable in such terrain.

When you have selected a spot for your pit, avoid disturbing the snow surface directly uphill from where you'll dig. Dig a hole about four feet across and about five feet deep or to the ground, whichever comes first. When the hole is done, smooth the uphill wall with your shovel. The wall should be as vertical as possible. Some questions you need answers for are: Is there a slab? What is its size (thickness and area)? How well is the slab bonded to the layers beneath it? What will it take to make the slab slide on the layer beneath?

A patroller tests the hardness of a layer in the snowpack.

Identifying Layers. Insert your plastic card vertically into the top of the pit wall. Slide the card down the wall and feel the relative resistance of the layers. Note the boundaries of hard and soft layers.

Layer Test. Lightly brush the pit wall, using your paint brush or a glove with horizontal strokes. The harder, stronger layers in the snowpack will stand out, while the softer, weaker layers will recede under the brushing. A very narrow ridgelike layer might be an ice crust, while a narrow recessed layer is most likely cohesionless and may be a sliding layer if it is between slabs. Slabs show as wider bands of raised surface.

Hardness Test. Gently push your hand into the side wall to test the hardness of each layer. A soft layer allows your whole fist to penetrate the snow, while a hard ice layer barely allows a knife to penetrate. Hardness can be classified as fist (very soft); four-finger (soft); one-finger (medium); pencil (hard); and knife (very hard). By now you should be forming an opinion about the layers you've found and their relationship to each other. The next test is where you see how cohesive the slabs are and how easily they slide (or don't slide) on the layers below them.

Shovel Shear Test. On the surface of the snow above the uphill pit wall, use your shovel to mark out a "U" shape with each leg of the "U" as wide as your shovel blade. Dig out the snow on both sides of the "U," but leave the back attached to the snowpack. Now carefully insert your shovel at the back of the column you've made, with the blade parallel to the front of the column. When you've buried the shovel blade, gently pry the shovel forward. If any slabs lie on weaker layers, they should shear off above the weak layer. The amount of force needed to shear a particular layer shows you how well or how poorly that layer is bonded. For example, if a layer shears off before you even pry on the shovel, that's a very unstable layer and could easily fail (avalanche). Conversely, if you have to pry hard, or your shovel handle digs into the column without shearing it, that's an indication of a stable, cohesive layer or snowpack.

If any layer does shear off easily, turn the block of snow over and examine the bottom surface. Take a few snow crystals on your plastic card, and examine them. If you have one, use your magnifying glass. If you can't find any poorly bonded crystals there, look at the top of the layer below the slab that sheared. Did the slab shear on a layer you found earlier, or was it a very subtle layer that would only appear in a shear test or an avalanche? Repeat the shovel shear test until you reach the bottom of your pit, noting where layers shear off. See if the sliding surfaces correlate with anything you found in your earlier tests in the side wall of the pit.

The force required to shear a column is rated as very easy, easy, moderate, hard, or very hard. Very easy and easy shears generally mean you have unstable conditions, while hard and very hard shears generally mean a stable, cohesive

A patroller performs the shovel shear test.

snowpack. Shear strength is only one indicator, though, and you should consider other factors such as the steepness of the slope and the amount of snow lying above the layer in question. Stability is relative to the amount of stress on the snowpack. A steep slope exerts more stress on the snowpack than a gentle slope, and two feet of new snow exert more stress than six inches of snow.

Ski Testing

Ski testing is a good way to evaluate the stability of slide paths where the consequences of a "ride" wouldn't be serious. Slopes with cliffs or rock bands, with suspected deep slab instability, or heavily loaded slopes are not ski tested. Shovels, avalanche beacons, and at least one partner are required for ski testing.

To ski test a slope, teams of two or more patrollers start above the starting zone (or top) of the slope in question. The first patroller starts across the top while the others watch him carefully. The ski tester traverses the starting zone, making jumping motions as he goes across. The traverses should be fairly fast – at least fast enough for the patroller to keep moving rather than hiking. When the first patroller reaches a safe position, he turns around so he can watch the next patroller. Each member of the team makes a slightly lower traverse than the previous one until all have crossed. The team continues back and forth across the slope this way until a good portion of the slope has been tested.

The purpose of ski testing is to observe the reaction of the new snow to the action of skis, and to release any thin slabs that may have formed since the last ski test or explosive test. Some things to note are fractures, collapsing noises, and hard surfaces. Fractures and collapsing noises are indications of instability within the snowpack. Hard surfaces indicate pockets of hard wind slab that may be found in some terrain on lee slopes. You need to distinguish these from wind-scoured areas of hard snow that generally aren't prone to avalanching.

Sometimes ski testing is more effective in releasing thin slabs than explosive testing. If a thin slab rests on a sliding layer but is cohesive (has tensile strength), explosives may only make holes in the snow. Imagine a sheet of paper. You can

A patroller starts a small slab avalanche while ski testing a slope.

pull on the edges with quite a bit of force and not tear it. Poking a large hole in the paper, as a bomb would in a slab, doesn't affect that strength very much. But if you cut the paper with scissors, as a ski track cuts a thin slab, the paper loses all tensile strength. The paper falls apart; a slab avalanches.

Explosive Testing

Explosive testing is used where ski testing would be impractical or dangerous to the patrollers. Heavily loaded slopes, inaccessible slopes, and slopes above cliffs are routinely tested with explosives rather than ski tested.

Ski areas use 75mm and 105mm recoilless rifles, hand-placed explosive charges, and a device called the Avalauncher for explosive testing. Hand-placed charges are widely used, but training in the use of artillery and Avalaunchers is limited to a few experienced avalanche workers, so in this section we'll simply describe the methods and materials used with hand-placed charges.

Explosive work is exciting, but it can also be dangerous and can cause a hearing loss. The danger lies in more than handling high explosives – hand-placing explosives often requires that you ski in or near avalanche paths. Few explosive accidents have occurred in avalanche hazard reduction, but several patrollers have died when buried by avalanches. The explosives used in avalanche hazard reduction work are relatively safe to handle if the proper procedures are followed. Safety must be kept in mind during all phases of explosive work. Obviously, one important rule is: *No smoking during any phase of explosive work.*

Jackson Hole patrollers fire a 75mm recoilless rifle for avalanche hazard reduction. *Wade McKoy photo.*

SKI PATROLLER

The explosives used most widely for hand placement are called primers or boosters, as their original purpose was to detonate less sensitive explosives such as ammonium nitrate/fuel oil mixtures. There are two types: cast primers and gelatin primers. Gelatin primers consist of a mixture of nitroglycerine and inert ingredients similar to dynamite, while cast primers are a mixture of TNT and PETN. Cast primers are easier to prepare than gelatin primers, but cast primers leave black marks in the snow that can later cause rapid melting. Gelatin primers are cheaper and leave no black marks. The detonating system uses safety fuse, a fuse lighter, and a heat-sensitive, nonelectric blasting cap.

Fuse.   The fuse is cut to burn for at least ninety seconds after ignition, giving you time to retreat to a safe location away from the explosion. Fuse ends must be cut squarely and cleanly. A fuse end cut improperly and then inserted into the end of the blasting cap leaves a gap between the fuse and the cap's flash charge, creating the possibility of a misfire.

Caps.   The blasting cap is crimped onto the end of the fuse with a special tool. Simple hand-held crimping tools resembling pliers are used widely. They have a cutting edge for cutting and trimming safety fuse, and one handle is

A cap and fuse are inserted into a bench crimper for crimping. Crimping pliers and a crimped cap on a fuse lie next to the operator's left hand.

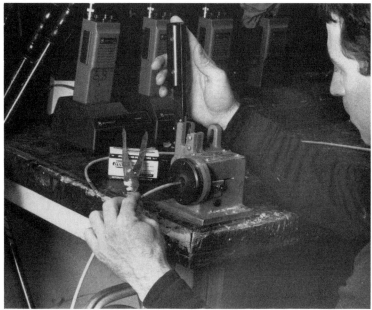

pointed for punching holes in gelatin primers or dynamite. The safest tool for crimping caps is the bench crimper. The bench crimper is solidly constructed to contain the blast of an accidentally detonated cap and is bolted to a bench. Crimping a cap wrong can cause it to detonate. The bench crimper also cuts fuse nicely by means of a replaceable blade mounted on the handle, and a guide helps square the fuse for cutting. With either tool the cap is placed over the end of the fuse. Then the cap is crimped at its base.

Assembling Fuse and Cap to the Primer.

Cast primers have two holes; one hole runs through the primer, whereas the other hole is slightly off-center and ends in the middle of the primer. The cap is inserted in the off-center hole, and the fuse runs out the full-length hole. The fuse and cap assembly is then taped to the primer. Gelatin primers have no holes, so holes must be punched in them. Two diagonal holes are punched, one clear through the primer, and one slightly deeper than the length of the cap. The cap is inserted in the short hole, and the rest of the fuse extends through the other hole. To prevent the cap from falling out of its hole, the fuse is taped on to either type of primer.

When the fuse and cap assembly is taped to the primer, the "bombs" are ready to go out on the mountain. When carrying bombs, take care to keep the fuse ends dry. Don't let them hang out of your pack or coat. Moisture on the end of a fuse can be driven down the burning fuse until it reaches the cap, where the moisture prevents the cap from igniting.

Fuse Lighters.

Fuse lighters must be carried separately from explosives. Never place fuse lighters in the same pack as your bombs. If you carry any bombs inside your coat, keep your fuse lighters in an outside pocket or let your partner carry them.

Explosive Placement.

Ideally, the charge should land where the slab would fracture if it avalanched on its own. Wind, fog, a rucksack, and heavy clothing all conspire to ruin your throwing accuracy. Sometimes the bombs land in the tops of small trees, and they can go straight up and land almost at your feet. Fortunately, the charges make enough of a bang to make pinpoint accuracy unnecessary. Experience and familiarity with the mountain will teach you the best places to aim your throws.

Lighting Fuses.

Before placing the fuse lighter on the fuse end, be sure everyone on your team is accounted for. Once the lighter has been placed on the end of the fuse, the bomb is fully armed and should be treated as if it were lit. In fact, the fuse can ignite as the igniter is placed on the end of the fuse. You can avoid this problem if you pull the wire out of the cardboard tube until you feel a slight resistance before putting the igniter on the fuse. Other things to be sure of before placing the igniter on the fuse end:

A patroller places the fuse lighter on the fuse. Note that the wire is not pushed all the way down into the lighter.

Know exactly where you will throw the charge.

Be sure everyone on your team knows where you will throw the charge and knows the escape route to a safe spot (a group of trees, behind the ridge line, and so forth).

Make sure all possible run-out zones are clear of skiers.

When all is ready:

1. Pull the wire out of the fuse lighter until you feel a slight resistance.
2. Place the bomb on the snow between your skis, or hold it between your knees. Be careful not to allow the fuse end to touch the snow. If any snow gets on the fuse end, brush it off. Some avalanche workers routinely cut a small piece off the end of the fuse before putting the igniter on. This assures a dry fuse end.
3. Push the igniter firmly down on the fuse end as far as it will go. The bomb is now armed and should be considered dangerous.
4. Hold the tube of the fuse lighter with one hand and give a sharp pull on the wire with your other hand. Quickly check to be sure the fuse is burning. Hold the end of the fuse lighter against the snow; if the fuse is lit, the smoke will make a dark spot in the snow. Also, the igniter will ride down the fuse slightly, while it won't on an unlit fuse. Your only other clues are a slight hissing noise (which you won't be able to hear in windy conditions), a small amount of smoke (which you may not be able to see in windy conditions),

Lighting the fuse – "Fire in the hole!"

and a slight darkening of the fuse. If in doubt, throw the bomb anyway, and throw it without delay in any case. An underhand toss is the most effective.

5. Retreat to your predetermined safe spot. Usually you'll still be close enough for the blast to be loud – cover your ears with your hands before the blast. Repeated exposure to blasting noise can result in permanent hearing loss.

Duds. If no explosion occurs within two minutes or more and you're using a ninety second fuse, it's likely you have a dud. You must attempt to retrieve or dispose of duds, but they shouldn't be approached for at least an hour. With cast

Just one blast this close can damage your hearing—cover your ears well before the bomb is due to explode. *Wade McKoy photo.*

primers, once you have waited an hour the fuse and cap can simply be removed from the primer. A new fuse and cap can be inserted and lit, or the primer can be kept unarmed and used another time. The other alternative is to dispose of the dud in place by placing another charge next to it. This can be tricky because of the difficulty of skiing into an avalanche path, lighting a charge, and then skiing to a safe spot. It's possible to throw the second charge and have it land close enough if you're a horseshoe pitching ace.

Rescue Beacons

As a precaution, all patrollers carry rescue beacons (avalanche transceivers) and shovels on avalanche hazard reduction routes. The beacons are often called "Pieps" or "Skadis," after two of the best-known brand names. Rescue beacons transmit a beeping radio signal when in the transmit mode, and receive that signal when in the receive mode. The closer you get to the transmitting beacon, the louder you hear the beep through the earpiece.

Always carry the beacon inside your coat, in the transmit mode, when you ski in avalanche terrain. To carry it in your rucksack or fanny pack is to risk having it torn from you in the turbulence of an avalanche. If someone on your team is caught and buried in an avalanche, all of you should switch your beacons to receive, and then proceed as follows:

1. Carefully note and mark the point where the victim was last seen. If there is danger of further avalanches, post an avalanche guard and be prepared to switch back to transmit.
2. Be certain all beacons are on receive. The leader should check this, as a single beacon left on transmit can frustrate the entire search.
3. Deploy a line of searchers at the level of the last-seen area and search downward. The spacing between searchers should not exceed 90 feet.
4. Keep the volume control turned all the way up until you receive a signal.
5. Move in unison, keep the line straight, and keep noise to a minimum. All searchers stop every ten paces and slowly rotate their beacons left and right, then front and back. Rotating the beacons orients them for the best signal. When you hear the strongest signal, hold the beacon in that position.
6. If you hear a signal, inform the group, but the line of searchers shouldn't be broken up. Orient the beacon for maximum signal strength. Turn the volume down until the signal can just be heard; the ear detects changes in loudness better at low levels. Don't change the orientation of the beacon while moving. This is very important because it causes false changes in signal level.
7. Stop at regular intervals to refine the orientation for maximum signal strength. Then reduce the volume. The best orientation will change as you get closer.
8. When the signal starts to get weaker, you have passed the victim. Scribe a line in the snow to mark this point.
9. Again orient the transceiver for maximum signal, maintain that orientation, and reduce the volume until the signal can just be heard. Now, back up until you pass the maximum signal point and the signal fades again. Mark this point in the snow. The two points bracket the victim's location.
10. Locate yourself halfway between the fade points. Orient the beacon for maximum signal strength. Then reduce the volume until you can just hear the signal. Search at right angles to the original search direction and establish fade points (B and B' in illustration). Continue systematically to improve the estimate of the victim's location. Three or four crisscrosses are usually enough.
11. It pays to pinpoint the position of the victim. Otherwise, you may have to move a great deal of snow, losing valuable time, before finding the victim.*

If you are the only searcher, the basic technique is the same. Begin at the last-seen point and work downward until you hear a signal. Then proceed as outlined above.

---

* *Avalanche Handbook,* 195–96.

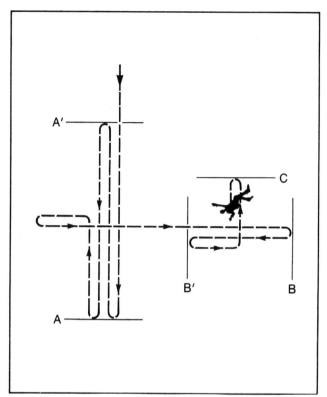

Avalanche beacon search pattern. *USDA Forest Service photo, from* Avalanche Handbook.

As mentioned earlier, few patrollers have died in explosives accidents, but several have died in avalanches. Few people realize that many patrollers survive avalanches. There are several reasons for this. The most important is that patrollers always work in teams and never expose more than one member of a team at a time to potential avalanches. If one member of the team is caught, there is at least one patroller standing by with a beacon and shovel, ready to search and dig.

Another reason patrollers survive is that they know what to do if caught. Along with wearing an avalanche beacon, a standard precaution is to ski without pole straps and use your hands to struggle to the surface of the snow or grab a tree, rock, or anything else that might stop your slide. It's also helpful to get your skis off and try swimming in the moving snow to stay on the surface. Thrusting one hand up to the surface while keeping the other hand near the chest and face to make a breathing space when the snow stops moving has saved several avalanche victims. Conserving oxygen by not struggling once the snow stops moving will also improve your chances of survival.

AVALANCHE FORECASTING

Organized Avalanche Rescues

Minimizing an avalanche victim's burial time is the key to any successful avalanche rescue. Most avalanche victims die of suffocation – brain damage begins four minutes after the brain is deprived of oxygen. Statistically, an avalanche victim buried for one half hour or less has a 50 percent chance of survival. Between half an hour and one hour, the chances are about 30 percent. After one hour, the victim's chances drop dramatically, although in April 1982 at Alpine Meadows, California, a woman was rescued alive after five days' burial in avalanche debris.

A late winter storm dropped a record-breaking fifteen feet of snow on California's Sierra Nevada during late March and early April of 1982. Avalanches closed roads, slammed into houses, and on March 31, 1982, a massive avalanche hit the base area of Alpine Meadows ski area. Several people were killed, including Mountain Manager Bernie Kingery. The continuing storm and avalanche hazard frustrated searchers for days, but on Monday, April 5, 1982, a German shepherd dog named Briget made history by becoming the first dog ever to find a live avalanche victim in the United States. Anna Conrad was saved by the fact that a row of lockers in the building she was in had fallen over her and kept the snow from completely surrounding her when the avalanche hit.

If an avalanche accident occurs near a ski area, chances are it can be reported to the ski patrol within five minutes. A quick response from a summit station by a small, well-equipped rescue team offers a good chance that the victim will be found within one half hour.

As a patroller, your role in an avalanche rescue will depend on your experience and your location at the time of the avalanche. Anyone who patrols at an area with avalanche potential, either in or out of the area, should be familiar with probing, organizing a probe line, and the other duties of the First Column Leader, as well as the duties of the Accident Site Commander and the Rescue Leader.

The First Column Leader. The first column is by definition the first group of searchers to go to the scene on an avalanche rescue. They are a hasty search team whose objective is to reach the accident site as quickly as possible.

The first column leader is responsible for screening volunteers, equipping them, instructing them in probing methods, and leading the column safely to the accident site. The first column travels light, bringing only the minimum equipment needed. A typical first column carries enough avalanche probes for each person, one or two sturdy snow shovels, flagging with which to mark their route for subsequent columns, and perhaps headlamps if darkness is near. Ideally, each column member is also equipped with an avalanche beacon. In areas where many skiers carry their own beacons, it may be practical to enlist only volunteers who do so. In most cases, though, the ski patrol will have to supply beacons.

As a first column leader, you must know what route you will take to the accident. After evaluating the danger of further avalanches along your route, if you feel your group is in danger, you will need to call for an avalanche hazard reduction team or choose an alternate route to the accident site. The safety of your column should be foremost – it will do neither you nor the accident victim any good if you become trapped by an avalanche on the way to a rescue. The first column leader acts as accident site commander until the designated accident site commander arrives. Usually someone with experience, such as the assistant ski patrol director, is designated accident site commander in the ski area's avalanche rescue plan, but that person is rarely on the scene before the first column leader. In the role of acting accident site commander, you decide where to search and brief and organize other columns as they arrive.

Probing For a Buried Victim. Before starting to probe, decide on the best starting point. Upon your arrival at the scene, you need to identify and prioritize the places where the victim is most likely to be. At the same time, decide if any danger of further avalanche remains. If a threat does remain, decide on an escape route and post an avalanche guard to warn of further avalanches. To determine the most likely search areas, follow these steps:

1. From the report of a witness or from tracks, determine where each victim entered the slide path.
2. If the witness knows, find out where each victim disappeared – the "last-seen area."
3. Determine the probable trajectory for each victim. In most cases, the victim will be carried by the moving avalanche down the "line of flow" from the last-seen area to the place of greatest snow deposition – usually the toe of the slide. The fall line (the line a ball would take if rolled down the hill) and the line of flow will usually be the same, but the momentum of the avalanche can alter the line of flow.
4. Using the above information, decide on the areas of highest search priority.

Once you have determined the areas of highest probability, conduct a rapid surface search of those areas. A "scuff search" is the quickest way to do this. In a scuff search, the searchers line up across the search area and scuff the surface of the snow with their boots. The locations of any clues should be marked, as any discovery of a glove, ski pole, or other equipment quickly narrows the search area.

If the victim isn't found during the scuff search, quickly organize searchers into a probe line. Probe highest probability areas first. As long as there is any hope of a live recovery, the quicker, if less thorough, coarse probe should be used. In a coarse probe, probers line up and space themselves by placing their hands on their hips and standing elbow to elbow. Probers then probe once between their feet on command from the probe line leader. On command they remove their probes, advance one short step, and probe again. As an alternative when few probers are available, probers can be spaced fingertip to fingertip. They then probe once in front of the left foot and once in front of the right foot. If a probe strikes something, the probe is left where it is and the line continues while a shoveler is assigned to dig. It's best to work uphill, as it is easier to maintain an orderly pace working uphill.

Probe line practice.

Coarse probing offers a 70 percent chance of finding the victim, as some thoroughness is sacrificed for speed. As long as there is a remote chance the victim will be found alive, the coarse probe should be used. Areas that have been probed should be marked to avoid overlapping and re-probing. After probing all likely areas with a coarse probe, it may be worthwhile to re-probe some areas with a coarse probe before resorting to the fine probe. The fine probe is almost 100 percent effective, but takes four or five times longer than coarse probing. The probes are inserted three times for each advance – once in front of the left foot, once in between the feet, and once in front of the right foot.

Accident Site Commander.   The accident site commander relieves the first column leader as soon as possible at the accident site. The accident site commander decides where to search and arranges probe lines, beacon searchers, and dog handlers as he sees fit. He uses a battery-powered megaphone to give instructions.

Rescue Leader.   The Rescue Leader is the overall coordinator of the rescue. The ski patrol director or assistant director will normally be rescue leader, but any patroller may be called on to be temporary rescue leader. The rescue leader arranges for manpower and equipment, including medical and air (helicopter) support. The rescue leader normally stays at a summit station and does most of his work by radio and telephone.

Avalanche Dogs

A well-trained avalanche dog can search an area 300 feet by 300 feet about eight times as fast as twenty probers can search the same area.* Many ski patrols keep avalanche dogs, and the dogs seem to earn their keep on their public relations value alone. Skiers often ask what the dog does, and that's an ideal chance for you to give some on-the-spot skier education in avalanche awareness.

In Europe, dogs are trained in avalanche rescue and kept available at the summit stations of many ski resorts. The number of avalanche accidents there makes it practical for dogs to be trained only in avalanche search. In the United States, the infrequency of accidents makes it impractical to have specialized avalanche dogs. The considerable investment in time and effort for training an all-around search dog is little more than for an avalanche dog. The dog and handler get more practice and experience by making themselves available year-round for lost-persons searches, disaster searches, plane crashes, and so forth. Many patrollers whose interest in dog handling started with avalanche rescue go on to train dogs for year-round lost-persons search.

Becoming familiar with all aspects of avalanches – forecasting, hazard reduction, and rescue – takes years of experience. But even a beginning patroller can share the awe and fascination of watching an avalanche run down a mountainside. The fascination may fade after years of fighting the weather and seeing people injured or even killed by avalanches, but the awe of being close to such a powerful force of nature remains.

---

* *Avalanche Handbook,* 196.

8

Mountain Sweep
and Other Short Subjects

T he first day of work on the mountain can be a disappointment for the new patroller who doesn't know what to expect. Visions of being the first to put tracks on the mountain for the season come crashing down with the reality of loading hundreds of pounds of rope, bamboo, and signs on the lifts or a snowcat, unloading them at the top, then loading them into toboggans and skiing along area boundaries and closed areas with a loaded toboggan. Then begins the slow work of unrolling rope and propping it up in the (usually shallow) snow with signs and bamboo. Depending on the ski area's size and the materials used for marking boundaries, a ski patrol will spend from one day to two weeks getting their mountain ready for opening. Then, after the last day of operation, all the rope, bamboo, and signs must be taken down and stored for the summer.

Rope and Bamboo Poles

The usual method of working when setting up rope boundaries and closed areas is for one patroller to ski along the intended line with a spool of rope while another drops signs and bamboo at the appropriate places. A third patroller pulls the toboggan loaded with materials; a fourth patroller ties the rope to the signs and bamboo and stands them up in the snow.

Bamboo is relatively fragile and will bend or break if not cared for. One way to avoid bending the bamboo used in boundary lines is to tie the rope to it by using a running clove hitch rather than simply wrapping the rope around the bamboo. Since the rope is run out before the bamboo is tied in, and in any case long lengths of rope are used, the conventional way of tying a clove hitch won't work. The running clove hitch works well and is a handy knot to know in ski patrol work. To form a running clove hitch, hold the rope between the thumb and fingers of each hand with your hands about one foot apart. Form a loop first in one hand, with the standing part of the rope crossing over the top part of the

Patrollers put up boundary ropes and signs before the skiing season begins.

loop. Form a loop on the other hand with the standing part crossing under the loop. Place the second loop above the first loop, then slide them onto the bamboo.

Rope and bamboo used for boundaries and closures need constant attention to remain effective. Snowstorms bury ropes and bamboo and coat them with rime ice, and rime ice adds more weight to a bamboo than it can support. If left heavily rimed, a bamboo pole will bend over and break. At a cost of $1 to $1.50 each, bamboo poles represent a considerable investment that every patroller

Tying a running clove hitch.

The running clove hitch tied to a bamboo pole.

should help to protect. With proper care, a bamboo pole should last two or more seasons.

The easiest way to remove rime ice from bamboo, rope, and signs is to hit them with your ski pole. One trick to remember: use the thicker handle end of the pole rather than the tip. Your ski poles will last much longer, as rime ice is hard and can easily break a ski pole at the thin end.

Once snow buries a rope, the rope becomes increasingly difficult to uncover. A buried rope leaves a gap in your barrier, and an unwary skier could ski over the rope into a closed area or out of the ski area boundary. If the rope isn't buried too deeply, your ski pole is a good tool to use for pulling the rope out. Again using the handle end, get your pole handle under the rope so the pole grip hooks under the rope. You can then ski slowly along the rope, sliding your pole along and pulling the rope out of the snow as you go.

Importance of Rope Boundaries

Many ski areas in the west are surrounded by avalanche paths, cliffs, and wilderness areas. Every year, skiers wander out of ski area boundaries, knowingly or unknowingly, and are buried in avalanches. Others become lost and are the

A ski patroller knocks rime ice off boundary ropes.

object of search efforts costing thousands of dollars. Well-marked ski area boundaries are the best prevention for these disasters and near-disasters, although some skiers refuse to be protected from themselves. It seems a few skiers will always ignore ski area boundaries or closed areas and become victims of avalanches. Many western states now have laws making skiing out of area boundaries or in closed areas punishable by law, and many ski patrols actively enforce those laws.

As more skiers search for untracked powder, ski area boundaries surrounded by tempting terrain can become a real headache for ski patrols. Enforcing closures becomes a game of cat and mouse with skiers, and catching offenders in the act can be difficult. Large resorts covering hundreds of acres of skiing terrain, and attracting thousands of skiers, give the ski patrol plenty of work more important than chasing out-of-bounds skiers. Smaller resorts may have their boundaries more visible from a central area, but small resorts also have proportionately small ski patrols, so there still may not be much time for patrolling boundaries and closed areas.

The issue is complicated by the fact that most western ski areas are surrounded by public lands and many operate on leased public lands. Proponents of out-of-area skiing argue that ski areas have no right to punish skiers who cross ski area boundaries, even if those skiers use the ski lifts to reach the boundaries they cross. But when skiers are buried and killed in avalanches, it is often the ski areas and local government agencies that bear the cost of rescue efforts.

At areas that do control boundaries, penalties for out-of-bounds skiing include a fine and a jail sentence in a few states. Elsewhere, there is no penalty unless the offender requires rescue services – then the penalty is payment of all rescue costs. Loss of skiing privileges for that day is the most common penalty for skiing in closed areas.

Hazard Marking

Marking potential hazards such as rocks, drop-offs, and holes on the slopes is a major part of a ski patrol's accident prevention efforts. Medium-sized rocks or bare spots can be effectively marked with bamboo stuck into the snow in an "X" pattern. Larger hazards such as cliffs or gullies may require rope, bamboo, and signs that say "Closed Area." Surveyors' wire "stake flags" are handy for marking small rocks or bare spots that probably wouldn't cause an injury but could damage a ski.

A good patroller is always on the lookout for potential hazards. If you are assigned a particular run for posting signs, part of your day should also include skiing that run to find potential hazards and mark them. You should also watch for bamboo or other hazard markings that may have fallen over or become partially buried in new snow.

To help protect skiers who might hit lift towers, most ski areas place pads or nets on the uphill side of their towers. The ski patrol is responsible for placing and maintaining these pads. Pads are made of a protective cover over a thick piece of foam padding. Nylon straps with buckles hold the pads in place. Patrols

Warning signs work most of the time, but some skiers choose to ignore them. This sign was written by the author and is posted above a cliff area at Grand Targhee.

that enjoy heavy annual snowfall pay for that luxury with the extra work of raising tower pads with every foot of new snow, then lowering them as the snowpack begins to melt in the spring.

Signs can warn skiers of potential hazards, and prevent skiers from getting into hazardous situations. Trail signs showing the relative degree of difficulty of a run can prevent skiers from skiing on runs above their ability. "Slow" signs (when skiers obey them) can prevent collisions or falls due to unexpected terrain changes. "Trails Merge" signs also help prevent collisions. Most ski areas consider signs a necessary evil, and signs increasingly dot the slopes. One ski patrol director joked that soon we'll need signs to warn skiers of the signs ahead.

Sweep

"Sweep" or "Clearing," the last run of the day, is the patrol's way of making certain no one is left injured on the mountain. All skiers must go down ahead of the patrol — you can't knowingly leave anyone behind you on sweep. A skier left behind might fall or be injured, and if that skier is skiing alone, no one would know until the next morning. By then the skier might die of hypothermia. Politely tell slow skiers that the mountain is being closed and that you must make sure no one is left on the mountain. Encourage them to keep moving — many skiers don't realize that you have other patrollers waiting for you. Sweep is also the time to put aside any signs that need to be out of the way of grooming equipment.

A ski patrol needs all its patrollers for sweep; in fact, the size of many ski patrols is determined by sweep requirements. If a late-afternoon accident call prevents you from helping with sweep, you should notify the patrol director as soon as you know you can't be available. The patrol director can then make arrangements for extra help to cover your sweep route.

When sweeping a run, you should ski slowly while looking all around, making wide passes back and forth across the run and stopping at regular intervals. Each time you stop, you should look for signs of movement that could be skiers, and for evidence of injured skiers among the trees. Each time you stop you should also yell "Sweep" or "Clearing," whatever term your ski area uses, then listen for any injured skier who might reply.

"X-ing" bamboo poles to mark an obstacle.

All ski patrols leave one or more patrollers at the summit or other patrol stations until sweep is completed, in case an injured skier is found on the mountain. The patrollers left behind, often called "supersweep," can then bring a toboggan for any injured skiers who might be found.

Sweep checkpoints at trail intersections and other strategic places help ensure that skiers can't ski into a run behind a patroller. If the patrol doesn't have radios, checkpoints also let patrollers keep track of one another as sweep progresses. If a patroller doesn't show up at his checkpoint within a reasonable length of time, that patroller may need help with an injured skier.

Sweep is not considered complete until all patrollers, including supersweep, are accounted for at the base area. Patrollers should stay in the patrol room until sweep is completed – anything can happen before that time. If supersweep gets hurt while coming down the mountain, someone will need to go back and assist the patroller who is injured.

Communications

Good communication is essential to the operation of a ski area and ski patrol. Most accident reports come from skiers who ski to lift stations or special telephones placed on the mountain for accident reporting, and accurate information is essential for a timely response to an accident call. Valuable time can be wasted

Two patrollers raise a tower pad.

A typical collection of spare signs and bamboo outside Sun Valley Ski Patrol headquarters.

when a patroller skis to the wrong location because of inaccurate information. Lift operators should have instruction on how to get information from skiers, and lift operators who ski and know the area can be a great help in getting accurate locations from skiers who report accidents.

Small ski areas may simply have one or two patrollers on duty at a summit station, and when an accident call comes in, those patrollers respond. In such a situation, without two-way radios it will be difficult to know what special first aid equipment is needed. The first patroller at the scene may have to assess the injuries, then send a bystander to a lift station to relay the information. If the accident site can be seen from the summit or toboggan station, simple arm signals can be used, at least to communicate whether a toboggan is necessary.

The ideal situation is for all patrollers to be equipped with two-way radios, and the summit or dispatch office equipped with a base station radio on the same frequency. Patrollers can then respond to accident calls from on the mountain rather than from a central station, and patrollers on the lifts or at the base area will know if their help is needed elsewhere. Also, one patroller can be dispatched to an accident without a toboggan; that patroller can radio back the exact location and say whether a toboggan or other first aid equipment is required. If an ambulance or helicopter is needed, patrollers can radio the dispatch office or summit and order one. This way, by the time the patient has been transported by toboggan to a transfer point, the ambulance or helicopter can be there or on its way.

Radio conversations should be kept short and to the point, especially when you're conveying information for an accident. You can't hear the other person while you talk on a two-way radio – you must stop transmitting and wait for the other person's reply. At many ski areas, other departments will be equipped with radios on the same channel as the ski patrol. In that situation, radio use becomes even more critical because more people may be waiting for you to finish your conversation so they can use the radio. Conversely, you may have to wait for another person to finish before you can use the radio. If you are handling a real emergency, you may have to break in and tell someone to wait until you can convey the essential information.

In the interest of keeping radio conversations short, to the point, and understandable, many terms used throughout this book may not actually be used by many patrollers in everyday conversation. Accidents are usually called "wrecks" except in accident report forms or other paperwork, and toboggans are commonly called "sleds." Patrollers dislike using words of more than two syllables anyway, and this may or may not reflect on the average intelligence of ski patrollers. When time is at a premium and you are talking over the radio, why say "We need a toboggan at the accident" when "We need a sled at the wreck" says the same thing in almost half the syllables?

The controls found on two-way radios are similar, no matter what brand they might be. They are the on/off/volume control switch, the transmit button, the channel selection switch, and the squelch control. The *off/on/volume control switch* turns the radio on and off and controls the volume of the receiver. The *transmit button,* usually located on the side of the radio, must be pressed before you attempt to transmit and should be protected from accidental pressure inside a coat pocket or elsewhere. Nothing is worse than having someone tie up a radio system unknowingly by having the transmit button pressed down while its carrier goes about skiing or working. No one else can use the system if this happens. Use the *channel selection switch* to set your radio to the correct channel. The squelch control eliminates static on the receiver when no useful signal is being received; it should be adjusted daily. Some radios have no squelch control. Others have a squelch control and a *private line switch.* The private line eliminates signals from transmitters that share your frequency but are too distant to give a strong signal. (Many unrelated two-way radio users operate on the same frequency band, and base-station transmitters have more power than hand-held sets.) The private line eliminates distant signals that might otherwise be received on your radio.

When talking over the radio, use a normal tone of voice. The radio is sensitive to sound, and shouting isn't necessary. In fact, speaking too loudly usually overpowers the microphone and your message may be garbled. Hold the radio a few inches from your mouth and speak slowly and clearly. If your area uses call numbers for individual patrollers, you should start every transmission with the call number of the person or station you want to reach, then your own call number. Some areas use the "ten-code" (ten-four means "Affirmative" or "Okay"; ten-twenty means "What's your location?" and so forth.) Some areas don't. Some areas use their own codes for different types of accidents; others prefer plain English.

Radios are delicate and require care to function properly. They should be protected from moisture and cold — moisture can ruin the speaker/microphone, and cold reduces battery power. On snowy days, radios shouldn't be carried outside your coat without some sort of protection—a plastic bag or a specially made nylon cover. An inside pocket is an ideal place to carry your radio.

Dropping a radio is a good way to cause it to be sent to the repair shop. Be careful when taking your coat off if you carry your radio in a coat pocket—the radio can easily fly out of the pocket and land on the floor. At the end of the day, radios should be turned off and placed in their battery chargers. Some batteries will last two or more days without recharging, but recharging takes from one to eight hours, so once the battery goes flat your radio is essentially out of commission for the day.

On a higher level, good communication means more than just exchanging accurate information such as locations and types of injuries. Patrollers often work in teams, especially on accidents, and good teamwork depends on communication and team spirit. In the interest of better patient care, constructive criticism among patrollers is very helpful after an accident case is finished. Maybe very minor operations could have been improved, but talking about them openly will give you and your partners honest feedback that may well help you handle the next "wreck" more efficiently. In the spirit of teamwork, there should be no reason to take criticism personally, and likewise, criticism should not be given in such a way as to single out one individual or to say, "It bugs me when you do that."

Following up on a patient's condition is a common ski patrol practice and is a form of good communication. Usually a patrol director or other supervisor makes the call. If a good relationship between the patrol and the hospital has been established, the patrol director can find out what a patient's actual injuries were, and the patrollers involved can compare that to the suspected injuries. Another common practice is for the patroller involved to call or write a note to the injured person, asking how he or she is doing, how the injury was treated at the hospital, and how the person's recovery is going. This shows genuine concern for the patient, and most injured people appreciate that kind of concern.

Sometimes you'll even get a thank-you card or see a skier you once rescued and get a hearty thanks in person. Just one thank-you from a skier you rescued can make your whole month. The thank-yous are the icing on the cake of a job that many people keep coming back to despite the aches and pains, the damaged and worn-out ski equipment, and the many small, thankless jobs that a patroller performs.

9

To Be or Not to Be
a Ski Patroller

On good ski days, professional patrollers, along with ski instructors, are the envy of the ski world. Skiers, ski area employees, and even some volunteer patrollers find themselves thinking, "Those guys have it made." And in some ways, pro patrollers do have it made. What could be better than skiing for a living?

What many people don't see, however, are the long hours patrollers spend in ski boots but not actually skiing. Nor do many people see the days when the skiing and the weather are miserable – most skiers can choose not to ski on those days – but the pro patroller has to be there, good weather or bad. When ski season ends, people with full-time careers keep on working and bringing home a paycheck; whereas many pro patrollers go out in search of a new job each spring.

But if you love skiing and enjoy helping other people, ski patrolling can be a rewarding career. If working at the same job year-round doesn't appeal to you – if you would enjoy the yearly change of jobs that most patrollers experience – then ski patrolling offers the freedom to pursue other jobs, even second careers, during the off-season.

Mixed emotions accompany many professional patrollers on that last sweep run of the season. They may be reluctant to see the ski season end for various reasons – maybe the skiing has been great, they've made new friends, or met an attractive member of the opposite sex. At the same time their feet or knees probably hurt, their savings accounts are bankrupt, and their faces have been fried by the sun. For weeks the talk over drinks after work has likely been, "What are you doing this summer?"

Vacations top everyone's list, of course. Baja California, Florida, Maui, the deserts, and whitewater rivers are popular places to unwind after a long ski season for those who can afford it. A trip to the hometown to visit friends and relatives also rates high among patrollers' post-season favorites. But when ski season and vacation time are both over and it's time to get serious about making some money again, pro patrollers must find a "real" job.

Employment Beyond the Ski Season

If making money is high on your list of priorities, think twice about making ski patrolling your profession. In 1989, starting salaries for professional patrollers ranged from $4.25 to $12 per hour. The average for experienced patrollers was about $7 per hour. Considering the cost of housing in most ski towns, beginning patrollers live on very low budgets during the winter or work an extra job at night. Working in a ski repair shop keeps patrollers close to what they know best – skiing – and many repair shops do their repair and tune-up work at night to provide customers with overnight service. Other second-job possibilities include waiter, bartender, dishwasher, or convenience store clerk.

Some pros have summer jobs waiting each year, while many others go out each year to find a new job. A few pro patrollers stay employed year-round at their ski areas as trail crew workers, blasters, or in lift maintenance and construction, and about one-third of the patrollers who responded to an informal survey said they work in construction during the summer. Another third are employed as river rafting guides, fishing guides, or tennis or golf pros.

The building trades are an excellent choice for those who like to stay close to home while making enough money to offset the typical pro patroller's low winter income. Highway construction also offers the chance to "catch up" financially, but employment is usually spread around the country, requiring you to follow the jobs and live in a trailer, camper, or motel. Construction work often requires a new job search each year.

The pro patrollers who don't work as guides or in construction fill an amazingly wide variety of jobs during the off-season. One Steamboat, Colorado, patroller works as a trapeze artist for Club Med during the summer. Another Steamboat patroller works as a crew member on pleasure charter boats in the Caribbean, while a third travels to Hawaii each year to work as a tour guide. One die-hard patroller even travels to New Zealand to patrol at a ski area there during summer in the United States. Patrollers also own businesses as building contractors, river rafting or fishing guides, and mountain bike tour guides.

Job-Related Benefits

Aside from the skiing, a career as a pro patroller offers a few job-related benefits that make life a little easier and more enjoyable. As mentioned in Chapter Two, manufacturers and retailers offer substantial discounts on ski equipment and clothing to pro patrollers. Normally you get a printed form, commonly called a "pro form," from your patrol director. The form lists the prices and models available from one manufacturer. Your ski patrol director must sign the form, certifying that you are a full-time professional; then you return the form to the retailer or to the manufacturer with payment. In some cases you take the equipment out of the retailer's shop on payment; in others you mail the form to the manufacturer with payment, and the equipment is shipped to you.

As a professional courtesy, many ski areas "comp" (issue a complimentary lift ticket) to visiting professionals from other ski areas. The practice isn't as common as it once was, partly because a few individuals have abused the system and partly because patrollers from areas that are located long distances from each other rarely get the chance to reciprocate. If you intend to visit another ski area while you're employed as a pro patroller, the best policy is to call or write the ski area you want to visit before going. Ask the patrol director if he "comps" patrollers from your area. Your patrol director will make the final arrangements. Be sure to thank your hosts, and if they invite you to visit with them in the summit shack or after skiing, by all means do so. "Comp" tickets are a courtesy to you and your ski area. They aren't a right to be taken for granted.

Patroller Exchanges

The best way to visit another ski area is by participating in a professional exchange. On professional exchanges, two patrollers from your ski area visit another ski area while two patrollers from that ski area come to yours. You get your usual salary, and the patrollers visiting your ski area get their usual salary. Most exchanges last five days, although closely neighboring areas may participate in shorter exchanges. Housing is arranged through the patrollers, and is often at patrollers' homes.

When skier safety is your goal, a free exchange of ideas benefits everyone. Patrol exchanges offer a chance to compare ways of doing things in a business where your nearest neighbor may be hundreds of miles away. Signs, fast-skier control, and skier education are subjects where new ideas can be borrowed to everyone's advantage.

"Exchanges are worthwhile," said Squaw Valley USA Patrol Director Mark Mueller, "because we tend to get 'tunnel vision' concerning our specific areas. Exchanges tend to encourage openness to new ideas and concepts." Squaw Valley USA has participated in exchanges since 1977.

Personal equipment, first aid techniques, and general working conditions also are hot topics on patrol exchanges. Trying out a new piece of gear at the resort you visit beats looking at a picture in a magazine article. The ski patrol at Bridger Bowl, Montana, actively pursues several exchanges each winter, and Bridger Bowl patrollers bring a two-carousel slide show of their area operations when they go on exchanges. Bridger Bowl patrol director Joel Juergens said, "We have stolen our best ideas of the last eight years from exchanges."

Relief from boredom is a valuable side benefit for patrollers who go on exchanges. Many patrollers become familiar with the vague lack of interest that is sometimes called "patrol burnout." A patrol exchange is a chance to ski another mountain and meet new people at minimum expense.

The idea for exchanges may have come from the cultural exchange and scholarship program practiced by university students and professors. Begun after World War II by Senator William Fulbright, the Fulbright Scholarship Program allows American students and professors to study in foreign countries while students from the participating foreign countries study in the United States.

A few American ski resorts participate in a program identical to the Fulbright Scholarship Program – Sun Valley, Vail, and Jackson Hole patrollers benefit from season-long exchanges with various resorts in France. Sun Valley has exchanged with Serre Chevailler, Vail with Courcheval, and Jackson Hole with Tignes and Méribel. The season-long foreign exchanges offer the experience of a lifetime for those lucky enough to take part. Patrollers with seniority, good attitude, and the most interest are a patrol director's first choice in deciding who goes on any exchange. For foreign exchanges, other factors include financial resources as well as knowledge of or interest in foreign languages.

Your Attitude

A good attitude goes a long way in any business, and in ski patrolling your attitude largely determines whether or not you will succeed as a professional patroller. Much of a patroller's work involves teamwork with other patrollers. No one wants to work with a partner who complains constantly or isn't willing to do his share of the work. Of course, everyone has bad days and human nature almost requires us to complain occasionally, but the patroller who shows a positive attitude towards his work will continue to advance and be a valued employee.

Working with other patrollers under sometimes stressful conditions – serious accidents, poor skiing, low pay, cramped quarters in the summit shack – tests the patience of even the most easygoing patrollers. It takes continuing effort on everyone's part to avoid major personality conflicts, and sometimes personalities must be set aside in order to make the patrol function as a team. In first aid work, you *must* be able to set aside any personal differences you have with the patrollers you work with. In the interests of good first aid and the welfare of the injured person, you cannot let personality conflicts interfere with patient care.

A "me first" attitude not only makes working with other patrollers difficult; it makes working with the skiing public difficult. As a representative of ski area management, you should always present a positive attitude to the skiing public. The ski patrol's job is to help skiers have a safer, more enjoyable skiing experience. Patrollers are not police officers, and few of the mistakes skiers make are crimes.

The Life of a Patroller

Many pro patrollers continue patrolling year after year despite the relatively low pay, and some continue despite knee injuries, close calls with avalanches, and all the other hazards that come with the job. A favorite saying of skiing great Otto Schniebs, Dartmouth's skiing coach during the 1930s, was: "Skiing is not a sport. Skiing is a way of life." In today's world, fewer and fewer skiers feel that way, but for professional patrollers, skiing and ski patrolling are definitely a way of life. Skiing every day in good conditions and bad, helping injured skiers, and making the mountain a safer place to ski – these features of the work form a bond among patrollers that often lasts a lifetime, even if the patrolling career doesn't. Each day presents the patroller with a new set of possibilities, and rarely are any two days alike.

The life of a pro patroller may seem unstructured, unprofitable, or even uncomfortable to some (notably the parents and in-laws of patrollers), but for most patrollers it's the only way to live. It could possibly be the best job in the world.

Glossary

Anemometer. A device for measuring wind speed.

Avalanche transceivers. Electronic devices used to locate a person buried in an avalanche.

Bastard search. A preliminary search for a lost skier to determine whether the person is truly lost. Places commonly searched at this stage are lodges, restaurants, bars, and restrooms.

Belayer. A person who controls a rope used to assist another person in making a gradual descent, as in lift evacuation or rock climbing.

Carabiner. A metal alloy link with a gate that permits insertion of a rope.

Cat track. A road or traverse used by snow grooming equipment ("cats" or "snow cats") and skiers to get from one part of a ski area to another.

Chair grip. The part of a ski lift that attaches the chair to the cable.

Cornice. An overhanging lip or block of snow formed by the wind.

CPR. Cardiopulmonary Resuscitation. A technique used to resuscitate victims of cardiac arrest.

EMT. Emergency Medical Technician. A person trained extensively in first aid, basic life support procedures, and automobile extrication.

Moguled slopes. Slopes with moguls (large bumps) from top to bottom.

Pieps. A brand name of avalanche transceiver.

Run-out zone. The bottom boundary of an avalanche path. Usually the area of greatest snow deposition.

Set up hard. A term for snow that has been groomed and had time to harden, has melted and refrozen, or has avalanched and been deposited in a run-out zone.

Sheave.   A rubber-lined, grooved wheel that guides a lift cable.

Starting zone.   The part of an avalanche path where the avalanche usually starts.

Sweep.   The ski patrol's last run of the day, when patrollers make sure no skiers are left on the mountain.

Tilled.   A term for snow that has been groomed with a "tiller," a device that grinds and smooths the snow surface.

WEC.   Winter Emergency Care. The National Ski Patrol's educational program of first aid for nonurban settings.

Further Reading

Chapter 1

Perla, Ronald, and M. Martinelli. *Avalanche Handbook.* Fort Collins, Col.: USDA Forest Service, 1976.

Chapter 2

Cooper, Christin. "How to Build Strength (Without a Lot of Heavy Apparatus)." *Skiing,* October 1985.

————. "Making Training Fun." *Skiing,* November 1986.

Enzel, Robert G. *The White Book of Ski Areas.* Washington, D.C.: Inter-Ski Services, Inc. Published annually.

Plisk, Steven. "Physical Conditioning for the Patrol Season." *Ski Patrol Magazine,* Spring 1987.

Chapter 3

Bowman, Warren D., Jr. *Outdoor Emergency Care.* Denver: National Ski Patrol, 1988.

The Ski Patroller's Manual. Denver: National Ski Patrol, 1985.

Chapter 4

Commins, Michael. "The Lowdown on the Showdown." *Ski Patrol Magazine,* Spring 1988.

Leppert, Alicia. "Equal Partners on the Patrol." *Ski Patrol Magazine,* Spring 1987.

————. "Mammoth Mountain: Skier Safety Program." *Ski Patrol Magazine,* Fall 1986.

————. "Skier Safety Education Workshop Recommendations." *Ski Patrol Magazine,* Winter 1986.

Leppert, Alicia. "Vail Aerial Tramway and Ski Safety Seminar Explores Skier Safety Education." *Ski Patrol Magazine,* Winter 1986.

Shealy, Jasper E. "How Dangerous Is Skiing and Who's at Risk?" *Ski Patrol Magazine,* Winter 1986.

Chapter 5

Gregory, John Forrest. *Rock Sport: Tools, Training, and Techniques for Climbers.* Harrisburg, Pa.: Stackpole Books, 1989.

Lift Evacuation Technical Manual. Denver: National Ski Patrol, 1982.

Loughman, Michael. *Learning to Rock Climb.* San Francisco: Sierra Club Books, 1981.

Robbins, Royal. *Basic Rockcraft.* Glendale, Cal.: La Siesta Press, 1982.

Roder, Hans. "Do the Prusik Two-Step Like an Inchworm." *Ski Patrol Magazine,* Fall 1984.

Wheelock, Walt. *Ropes, Knots, and Slings for Climbers.* Glendale, Calif.: La Siesta Press, 1986.

Chapter 6

Bryson, Sandy. *Search Dog Training.* Pacific Grove, Calif.: Boxwood Press, 1984.

Lavalla, Rick, Skip Soffel, Bill Wade, and Jim Brady. *Search Is an Emergency.* Tacoma, Wash.: The Emergency Response Institute, 1981.

Chapter 7

Fesler, Doug, and Jill Fredston. *Snow Sense: A Guide to Evaluating Avalanche Hazard.* Anchorage: Alaska Department of Natural Resources, Division of Parks and Outdoor Recreation, 1984.

————. "Stability Evaluation" in *National Avalanche School Textbook.* Reno, Nev.: National Avalanche School, 1985.

LaChapelle, E. R. *The ABC of Avalanche Safety,* 2d ed. Seattle: The Mountaineers, 1978.

Perla, Ronald, and M. Martinelli. *Avalanche Handbook.* Fort Collins, Col.: USDA Forest Service, 1976.

Williams, Knox, and Betsy Armstrong. *The Snowy Torrents.* Jackson, Wyo.: Teton Bookshop Publishing Company, 1984.

Index

Clothing
  choosing, 26
  search and rescue, 88, 89
  ski gloves, 25–26, 88
  See also Equipment
Clove hitch, running, 117–18, 119
Communications
  importance of, 124–25, 127
  public relations, 62–63
  radio, 125–27
Conditioning, physical, 21–22
Conrad, Anna, 112
Cooper, Christin, 59
Cornice cutting, 5
CPR (cardiopulmonary resuscitation),
  29, 30
  mask for, 35
  in a toboggan, 46–48
Crystal Mountain (Washington), 38
Crystal toboggans
  description of, 38
  handling of, 44, 52

Death/injury statistics, 57
Deer Valley (Utah) ski patrol, 63
Diaper sling, 79, 81–82, 83
Dogs, search, 85, 86
  for avalanche searches, 90–91,
    92, 115
  choosing and training, 90–93, 115
Dole, C. Minot, 18–19, 57
Duds, 108–9

Edson, Frank, 18–19, 28
Ellington, Wayne, 79
Emergency Medical Technicians (EMTs),
  28, 30, 31
Enforcing rules, 55, 59–62, 121
Enzel, Robert G., 21
Epley, Dick, 91
Equipment
  evacuation, 35, 74–76, 79, 81–82
  first aid, 28, 31–35
  search and rescue, 89–91
  ski, 22–27
  See also Toboggans
Evacuation, lift
  cost of gear for, 35
  knots for, 66–74
  light line for, 76
  plans for, 83–84
  rock climbing methods, 77–79
  rope techniques, 66–67, 76,
    77–79, 80
  self-, 35, 65–67, 79–83

slings, 75–76, 79, 81–82, 83
tees, 75, 77
Exchanges, patroller, 131–32
Explosive testing, for avalanche hazard
  reduction, 2–5, 109
  assembling fuse and cap to the
    primer, 106
  caps, description of, 105–6
  carrying fuse lighters, 106
  description of, 104–5
  duds, 108–9
  fuse, description of, 105
  lighting fuses, 106–8
  placing explosives, 106

Fanny packs, 34–35
Fencing
  rope-and-bamboo
    boundaries/closures, 117–18,
    120–21
  traffic-control (speed traps), 59–61
Figure-eight bend, 69
Figure-eight knot, 67, 68
Figure-eight on a bight, 70, 72
First aid
  American Red Cross Advanced First
    Aid Course, 30–31
  arriving at the accident scene, 40–41
  CPR (cardiopulmonary resuscitation),
    29, 30, 46–48
  Emergency Medical Technicians
    (EMTs), 28, 30, 31
  equipment, 28, 31–35
  first aid room procedures, 48–51
  range of situations faced by patrollers,
    29–30
  toboggan handling, 18, 38–48
  Winter Emergency Care (WEC) course,
    20, 31, 48
First column leader, 112–13
Fisherman's knot, 68, 69
Forecasting and record keeping,
  avalanche, 95–99
Fulbright, J. William, 131
Fulbright Scholarship Program, 131
Fuse(s), explosive
  assembling fuse and cap to the
    primer, 106
  carrying fuse lighters, 106
  description of, 105
  lighting, 106–8

Garbage bags, 35
Gauze pads, 35
Gear. *See* Equipment

Snowpit tests, 99–100
  hardness test, 100, 101
  identifying layers, 101
  layer test, 101
  shovel shear test, 101–2
Snowplow technique, 17, 20, 42, 43
Solitude (Utah) Ski Area, 49
Speed traps, 59–61
Splints
  backboards, 33–34
  cardboard, 30, 31
  Hare traction, 33
  inflatable, 32
  quick, 31
  removal of, 49–50
  Sager traction, 33, 34
  Thomas half-ring, 33, 34
  traction, 33, 34, 49
  vacuum, 32–33
  wing, 32
Squaw Valley USA (California) ski
  patrol, 131
Standards required of patrollers, 19–20
Steamboat (Colorado), 130
Stowe (Vermont), 18
Sunblock, 26–27
Sunglasses, 27
Sun Valley (Idaho), 36, 37
  ski patrol, 131–32
Sun Valley toboggans
  description of, 36, 37, 38
  handling of, 38, 44, 51
Sweep, 14–15, 122–24
  super-, 124

Tape, adhesive, 35
Tees, evacuation, 75, 77
Tests, avalanche. *See* Avalanche hazard
  reduction

Tests, skiing skills, 19
Thomas half-ring splint, 33, 34
Toboggans
  Akia, 37, 38, 39, 44–45, 52
  Cascade, 36–39, 42–44, 46
  Crystal, 38, 44, 52
  handling of, 18, 38–48, 42–47, 49
  modern wooden, 35–36
  old-fashioned wooden, 27, 35
  returning to service, 51–53
  special handling techniques, 45–48
  Sun Valley, 36, 37, 38, 44, 51
  "Tony's Flight," 57–59, 61
Traction splints, 33, 34, 49
Traffic control
  fencing for (speed traps), 59–61
  signs for, 55, 59–61, 122, 125
Triangular bandages, 35
Turns, skiing. *See* Skiing skills

Vacuum splint, 32–33
Vail (Colorado) ski patrol, 131–32
Vests, 34–35, 36
Videos, safety, 57–59, 61

Water knot (overhand bend), 68
White Book of Ski Areas, The (Enzel), 21
Wing splint, 32
Winter Emergency Care (WEC) course,
  20, 31, 48
Winter Park (Colorado) ski patrol, 19,
  61, 62

Zdarsky, Mathias, 17